Your Kingdom Come

Gerard W. Hughes ◆ Sheila Cassidy
Peter Selby ◆ Annabel Shilson-Thomas
Karl Gaspar ◆ Jim O'Keefe

Your Kingdom Come

Reflections on the
Scripture Readings for Lent

DARTON·LONGMAN+TODD

The CAFOD/DLT Lent Book 1997

First published in 1996 by

CAFOD
Romero Close
Stockwell Road
London SW9 9TY

Darton, Longman and Todd Ltd
1 Spencer Court
140-142 Wandsworth High Street
London SW18 4JJ

Editor: Harriet Paterson

ISBN 0 232 52208 1

Cover photograph: Sean Sprague – children at Palm Sunday
celebration, Shinyanga, Tanzania.

Bible quotations are taken predominantly from the Jerusalem
Bible, published and copyright © 1967, 1968, and 1969 and the
New Jerusalem Bible, published and copyright © 1985 both by
Darton Longman and Todd Ltd and Doubleday and Co Inc.

Printed by Flexiprint Ltd
1 Aspen Court
Churchill Industrial Estate
Lancing, West Sussex BN15 8UN

Contents

About the authors

Sheila Cassidy, writer, lecturer, preacher and broadcaster and former Medical Director of St Luke's Hospice in Plymouth, is now a palliative care physician at Plymouth General Hospital. In 1975 she was tortured in Chile for treating a revolutionary - an episode which she recounts in her autobiographical work *Audacity to Believe*. Her experience in caring for the dying has informed her other much acclaimed works, amongst them, *Sharing the Darkness, Good Friday People* and most recently, *The Loneliest Journey*.

Karl Gaspar is a Filipino poet, playwright, novelist, theologian, songwriter, teacher, development worker and human rights advocate. A prisoner of conscience from March l983 to February l985 during the Marcos dictatorship, he became a Redemptorist brother upon release, helping to conduct missions in Mindanao. His jobs have included Executive Secretary of the Philippine Business for Social Progress and development officer of the National Secretariat for Social Action, Justice and Peace. He has long been one of CAFOD's key partners in the Philippines.

Gerard W. Hughes SJ, author of the spiritual classics *In Search of a Way, God of Surprises* and *Walk to Jerusalem*, has done much to help his readers honestly to explore the mysteries of the Christian faith. He now works on the development of a spirituality for people who are active in justice and peace work, and is based in Birmingham.

Jim O'Keefe is currently President of Ushaw seminary, having worked there in the past as Pastoral Director. He was director of Catholic Care North East for seven years and was then closely involved in setting up the Catholic Agency of

Social Concern (CASC). He has travelled widely through the developing world, amongst landless and indigenous peoples in Brazil, Central America, the Philippines and Africa. Recent writings include a short introduction to Catholic social teaching, *I'll Tell You a Secret*, published by CAFOD.

Peter Selby currently holds the William Leech Professorial Fellowship in Applied Christian Theology at Durham University. He spent most of his ministry up to 1984 working in the fields of Christian adult education and mission, and then spent nearly eight years as Area Bishop of Kingston, South-West London. He has written a number of books, the two most recent being *Belonging – Challenge to a Tribal Church*, and *Rescue: Jesus and Salvation Today*.

Annabel Shilson-Thomas works for CAFOD as a writer and editor. She has worked in publishing for a number of years and has written several children's books, including *A First Puffin Picture Book of Bible Stories* and *A First Puffin Book of Stories from World Religions*. She is married to an Anglican priest and herself served as an Anglican curate for four years.

Introduction

In a busy, frenetic world, Lent can be an oasis of calm, an opportunity to pause and reflect. Lent is a time when less is more. The church is stripped back of its decoration and we leave aside some of the things of the world in order to enter into a spirit of fasting, prayer and conversion.

Once some of these externals are cut away, there is an opportunity to focus on the essentials of our faith, to get back to the bedrock of our spiritual lives. Most of us make an effort during Lent to carve out more time for thinking about God, for prayer and for reading scripture.

However, what starts as a good intention can easily get pushed aside, so it can be helpful to have a starting point. The writers brought together here do not pretend to have any definitive answers, but they offer reflections on the readings for each day of Lent in the hope that these will act as catalysts for our individual thoughts and prayers.

Although they come from different backgrounds and countries, all these writers have first-hand experience of working with people in need. But whether referring to the poor in the Philippines or to ex-convicts in inner-city Glasgow, all of them encourage and challenge us to set aside time for God and to join with the poor in a spirit of justice and solidarity.

It is not only in the twentieth century that many experience difficulty finding space and stillness – Jesus and his friends had the same problem. Jesus went into the desert before his ministry began, perhaps because he foresaw that this would be his last opportunity for an extended period of solitude and reflection to prepare himself for what lay ahead. From then on, he would be in the thick of things.

Indeed, recognising the importance of retreat, Jesus encourages his apostles to draw aside when they return from their first mission. His compassionate words offer real respite to all exhausted spirits: "Come away to some lonely place all by yourselves and rest for a while" (Mark 6:31).

Unfortunately, life does not slow down to let Jesus or the apostles take a break. The crowds demand their attention, and once more work goes on until late. Jesus then tries again to withdraw, going off into the hills to pray, on his own this time, but before long he sees his friends in trouble in their boat and goes to rescue them.

Prayer is essential, not something that should be "fitted in" to a busy schedule if time allows. But if someone needs our help urgently then that must come first. These reflections for Lent make particular reference to the experience of the poor, at a time in the Church's year when we are especially called to do something about the suffering of those in need.

Gerard W. Hughes
Ash Wednesday to Saturday after Ash Wednesday

Ash Wednesday

A change of direction

Jl 2:12-18; Ps 50:3-6, 12-14, 17; 2 Co 5:20-6:2; Mt 6:1-6, 16-18

"Turn to the Lord your God again,
for he is all tenderness and compassion,
slow to anger, rich in graciousness,
and ready to relent."

(Joel 2:13)

One Thursday following Ash Wednesday, while I was working in Glasgow, a man burst into my room. He explained, breathlessly, that he had just been released from Barlinnie prison where he had not received the ashes, and asked if he might receive them now. I marked his forehead with cigarette ash, the only ash at hand, saying as I did so, "Remember thou art dust, and unto dust thou shalt return". He departed, his mind at rest.

In Catholic churches, Ash Wednesday often draws a larger congregation than the average Sunday. The symbolism of ashes on the forehead exerts a strong attraction over people. Symbols can fascinate us even when we are unaware of their meaning, as though our subconscious were more intelligent than our conscious mind.

Ashes on the forehead symbolise not only our mortality, but also our total dependence on other people and on other things at every moment of our existence. They remind us that we are in the hands of some power much greater than ourselves. Receiving the ashes on our forehead is a dramatic outer sign of an inner truth – that in God we live and move and have our being.

Lent is a time for focusing our attention on this truth, and for making it an influence on every aspect of our lives. On any journey to a particular destination, the destination obviously determines the direction in which we travel and underlies every decision we make on the way. From God we come, to God we return: our life is a journey, and every decision we make in life has an impact on the way we are going. That is why Lent is called a time of penance. Penance means a change of mind and heart, a change in the way we see and relate to people and things around us, a change of direction.

Thought for the day

As Lent begins, are we ready and willing to take a new direction in our lives, or are we perhaps too stuck in our ways to make real changes?

Prayer

God, from whom I have come and to whom I am returning, let me know your tenderness and compassion for me and for all creation. May this truth determine every decision I make.

Amen.

Thursday after Ash Wednesday

Share the load

Dt 30:15-20; Ps 1:1-4,6; Lk 9:22-25

"Unload your burden onto the Lord and he will support you."

(Antiphon for today's Mass)

Today's Mass antiphon may seem a surprising piece of advice for the beginning of Lent. We are so accustomed to thinking of Lent as a time for penance, which it is, and of penance as being a burdensome task, which it is not, that we rather expect an exhortation at the beginning of Lent to exclaim: "Bear your burdens courageously, and add on a few more voluntarily, for that will not only please God, it will also be good for you"!

In fact, to "unload your burden onto the Lord" is a way of doing penance, for it is to change the way we perceive God and life's burdens. Once we start seeing differently, we begin acting and reacting differently as well.

I once lived in a house on a hill overlooking the beautiful Clwyd valley. Whenever I felt irritable or angry, disappointed or sad, I used to hurl the irritability or sadness out of the window. The valley did not darken or explode in consequence: it remained exactly as it was, and meanwhile I felt much better. The valley became for me a symbol of God.

When I hand my burden over, I quickly realise how stupid I have been in carrying it for so long. I also begin to see that my burden can preoccupy me to the point where I am incapable of seeing much else. When my burden is heavy, I am unlikely to be concerned about other people's burdens, however crushing they may be, for I am totally absorbed in myself and my own pain. That is why justice and peace issues are not popular in most Christian churches, whereas the healing of memories and the healing of life's hurts are likely to draw the crowds.

If we cast our burden on the Lord, we begin to realise that God is not remote but is, in St Augustine's words, "Closer to me than I am to myself". I am not the centre of the Universe: God is. God shares our burdens, weeps within us, is our rock, refuge and strength. This releases us from one of the greatest burdens of all – our own sense of self-importance.

Thought for the day

Doing penance shouldn't have to be a chore – it is a way of getting closer to God.

Prayer

God, closer to me than I am to myself, enlighten me so that I can recognise you in every detail of my life. Let me know the freedom and joy that comes from unloading my burdens onto you.

Amen.

Friday after Ash Wednesday

Hearts of stone

Is 58:1-9; Ps 50:3-6, 18-19; Mt 9:14-15

Is not this the sort of fast that pleases me
– it is the Lord who speaks -
to break unjust fetters
and undo the thongs of the yoke,
to let the oppressed go free ...
to share your bread with the hungry,
and shelter the homeless poor.

(Isaiah 58:6-7)

Strange though it is, we can become very attached to our burdens! One psychologist, writing on depression, maintains that we only remain in depression because we find some advantage in that state: it can often save us from having to face something that we fear even more.

Lent can be a dangerous time for the soul. We can become very attached to our extra prayer, fasting and almsgiving, to the things we have given up: we become absorbed in our own observances. The prophets warn us against this absorption with ourselves and our own burdens, whether they are inflicted upon us or are self-imposed.

At the moment when we finally decide to hand over our burdens to God, we may well begin to see that our burden was a way of escaping from other much more serious responsibilities. I heard once of a man who suffered severe scruples on money matters. Whenever he took a bus or train journey he was plagued with doubts as to whether he really had paid the right fare. His scruples were a form of escape from a much more serious responsibility: at the time he was neglecting his poor and ageing parents.

The things we do as individuals can often have wider implications for our behaviour as a nation. The prophetic call to repentance is always made to the nation, not to the individual. The God to whom we turn is a God of compassion, who is concerned with all peoples, not just one country. As a nation, we are over-preoccupied with the health of our own economy. Keeping the financial markets running profitably can mean less food and shelter for our own poor, and that of other nations, as money from welfare and aid projects is re-routed into other areas. As long as we pursue such policies, our prayers and fasting are displeasing to God.

Thought for the day

No amount of prayer or penance will help us to grow if we are using this as an excuse to ignore the poverty and injustice right under our noses.

Prayer

God, take away our hearts of stone and give us hearts of flesh instead. Help us to reflect some of your immeasurable goodness and compassion in our own lives.

Amen.

Saturday after Ash Wednesday

Privatising religion

Is 58:9-14; Ps 85:1-6; Lk 5:27-32

If you do away with the yoke,
the clenched fist, the wicked word,
if you give your bread to the hungry,
and relief to the oppressed,
your light will rise in the darkness,
and your shadows become like noon.

(Isaiah 58:9-10)

The covenant which God made with Israel demands that Israel should mirror the compassion and tenderness of God in all her dealings, not only within the nation, but also with the stranger. In St Luke's account of the Sermon on the Mount, Jesus says, "Be compassionate, as your heavenly Father is compassionate." Most of the Old Testament Law is concerned not with ritual and religious observance, but with the way Israelites should relate to each other and to the stranger.

It is interesting that in Jesus' account of the Final Judgement, he makes no mention of religious rituals and practices. Our relationship with God is expressed through our relationships with each other: "I was hungry and you gave me to eat, thirsty and you gave me to drink ..." and so on.

This is a challenge to all of us which threatens to take us right out of our comfort zones: we may wish God had ordained things otherwise, but there is no escaping the awkward truth that loving God starts right here and now with our attitudes to our enemies, to the poor and homeless on our streets, to people whose races or religions we may not feel at ease with. One writer – and I hope he is wrong but have a nasty feeling that he is not – said that we are as near to God as we are to the person we like the least!

We have privatised our religion so successfully that religious people who campaign against nuclear deterrence, the arms trade, Third World debt, unemployment or homelessness can be accused by other religious people of meddling in matters which have nothing to do with them! It's extraordinary, but it often happens.

In churches, so much of our financial resources are spent in maintenance of Church buildings for the benefit of its members, and so much of our energy is expended in inner wrangling about the minutiae of variations in doctrine or liturgy, that any mention of the hungry and homeless millions can end up being sidelined as an irrelevance.

Thought for the day

When Jesus tells us to love each other, he is in fact asking us to do something very simple. It is only through our own closure and prejudices that this becomes so difficult.

Prayer

God, we beg you, give us a still heart and an open mind as you lead us from the prison of our individual and national preoccupations into the freedom of your universal kingdom.

Amen.

Gerard W. Hughes
First week in Lent

First Sunday of Lent

A risky business

Gn 9:8-15; Ps 24:4-9; 1 P 3:18-22; Mk 1:12-15

God spoke to Noah and his sons, "See, I establish my Covenant with you, and with your descendants after you; also with every living creature to be found with you, birds, cattle and every wild beast with you: everything that came out of the ark, everything that lives on the earth."

(Genesis 9:9-10)

Penance means a change of mind and heart. Real change means digging deep into our most firmly-held convictions, to examine whether they really are compatible with our Christian beliefs.

As individuals and as a nation we are averse to change; for example, many of us – Christians though we are – still support the possession of nuclear weapons and the principle of nuclear deterrence despite everything we know about the colossal destruction that these weapons could cause.

Do we really consider the risk of mass annihilation and lasting ecological disaster preferable to the mental upheaval involved in changing our minds? Many will find this question rash and provocative, and disagree violently with its implications, yet it is a question that must be asked. Surely our fundamental commitment to human life and God's creation must be a seamless garment.

As Christians, do we really believe that God's covenant is with all creation, with every living creature? Do we really believe that God is in all things, in all events? If so, do we see all events, all crises as God's invitation to us to change? When we refuse to change, whose kingdom are we preserving, God's or our own? What is the basis of our belief, is it faith in God at work in all peoples and in all things, or is the basis of our belief that to which we have grown accustomed and in which we feel secure?

This obstinate refusal to change characterises our lives, both secular and religious. It is even true of some aspects of the Church. "What", goes the question, "is the difference between a liturgist and a terrorist?" And the answer is: "You can negotiate with a terrorist"!

As Christians we must pray for a spirit of repentance for ourselves and for the whole Church. If we truly became filled with that spirit, just think of the changes that could happen. In the first place, all the barriers between the different Christian denominations would surely come crashing down. Then this newly united Christian people would kick up a genuine political rumpus by insisting that economic and political decisions take account of the real values of God's covenant. Ruthlessly looking out for our national interest is not enough; our decisions should mirror the compassion and tenderness of God for all creation.

Thought for the day

God has put us in charge of creation on Earth. It is a responsibility we cannot take lightly.

Prayer

God, open our minds and hearts to the reality of your presence in all peoples and in all things so that we can recognise that what we do to any other person, we are also doing to ourselves and to you.

Amen.

First Monday of Lent

Practical Holiness

Lv 19:1-2, 11-18; Ps 18:8-10, 15; Mt 25:31-46

The Lord spoke to Moses; he said: "... Be holy, for I, the Lord your God, am holy."

(Leviticus 19:1-2)

Under the entry "spiritual", Collins English Dictionary gives the following definitions: "1. Relating to the spirit or soul and not to physical nature or matter; intangible. 2. Of, relating to, or characteristic of sacred things, the Church, religion, etc." Under the entry "holy" it gives: "of, relating to, associated with God or a deity; sacred."

When we hear the word "holy" applied to a person, what kind of person do we envisage? Would you like to go on holiday with such a person or live in the same house as them? Biographers of holy men and women usually emphasise the hours they spend in prayer, their fasting feats and tough ascetic practices; reading the lives of the saints can leave us with the impression that God is best pleased with us when we are punishing ourselves.

However, God himself gives an alternative explanation to the Israelites of what he means when he tells them to be holy. They must not steal nor deal deceitfully or fraudulently with their neighbour. They must not swear falsely using God's name. They must not exploit or rob their neighbour, deprive labourers of their wages or deliver unjust verdicts. They must neither be partial to the little person nor be overawed by the great. They must not slander their own people nor jeopardise another person's life. They must not harbour hatred of another in their hearts, but should instead tell each other openly of their offences. They must not exact vengeance, but must love their neighbour as they love themselves.

What a marvellous description of holiness, so down to earth, so obviously practical! This set of rules is just as relevant and functional today as it was thousands of years ago – God's law continues to make perfect sense, whether interpreted in a religious or in a social context. Prayer and ascetic practices should not replace these down-to-earth principles but rather be a way of focusing on them, giving us the strength to carry them into all our daily dealings.

Thought for the day

Through prayer we are reaching out to God, but through the daily practise of being holy men and women we can reach out to those around us as well.

Prayer

God, cleanse our minds of false images that we may have of you or of what holiness means, so that we may find you, and our own salvation, through loving and helping each other.

Amen.

First Tuesday of Lent

The word at work in us

Is 55:10-11; Ps 33:4-7, 16-19; Mt 6:7-15

Thus says the Lord: Yes, as the rain and the snow come down from the heavens and do not return without watering the earth, making it yield and giving growth to provide seed for the sower and bread for the eating, so the word that goes from my mouth does not return to me empty, without carrying out my will and succeeding in what it was sent to do.

(Isaiah 55:10-11)

Many different images are used to represent the word of God in the Bible. Jesus compares it to seed falling onto the ground; Paul in his letter to the Hebrews describes it as a two-edged sword which penetrates between the bone and the marrow. Today's passage from Isaiah compares the word of God to the rain which falls on the earth bringing growth.

The most dramatic account of all, however, of the power of God's word is found in the opening verses of Genesis. Each of these begins: "God said ..." and goes on with devastating simplicity to show that what God says, happens. "God said, 'Let there be light', and there was light."

The word of God is active and life-giving; it is an overwhelming force. We hear this again and again, and in principle we may piously believe it, but how are we to experience it in a real way during our daily lives? Prayer is one of the best ways of letting the word of God rain down upon us, work within us, change and transform us, so that God's loving purpose for all creation can be fulfilled in us and through us.

The seed and the rain fall upon the earth. It is extraordinary that we have developed such unearthly ideas about prayer that the last thing we want is to let the word of God fall on our earthiness, on our everyday preoccupations and activities. We tend to regard this as a "distraction", and try to banish it from our minds. This enables us to keep God from interfering in our lives, whether private or national, so that we are not disturbed from our set patterns of thought and behaviour.

We should be much more careful about dismissing the everyday things that tend to crowd into our mind when we are trying to pray. If we present our "distractions" to God in prayer, we may well find that surprising things happen.

Thought for the day

Prayer is not a private hobby for the more devout. It is a cosmic process of two-way communication in which we are all invited to co-operate.

Prayer

Father, may your kingdom come in us and through us. Teach us how to pray so that your life-giving rain can heal and nourish the dry roots of our hearts.

Amen.

First Wednesday in Lent

Take off your shoes

Jon 3:1-10; Ps 50:3-4, 12-13, 18-19; Lk 11:29-32

"On Judgement day the men of Nineveh will stand up with this generation and condemn it, because when Jonah preached they repented."

(Luke 11:32)

"You are precious in my eyes and I honour you," (Isaiah 43). Although we may find this statement hard to believe, it is a very effective Lenten exercise to focus on these words in our prayers, hearing God speak to us and encourage us. Reflecting on them can fill us with feelings of life and freedom and help us to become "the goodness of God".

This is not just an individual gift to ourselves alone, but something that extends through the goodness of God to every human being and to the whole of creation. Today's readings from the prophet Jonah and from St Luke's gospel emphasise the universality of God's love and condemn those who try to privatise it, reserving it for a chosen élite.

Jonah, called by God to preach to the wicked people of Nineveh, tries his best to escape from the responsibility, but God gets him to Nineveh anyway – via whale transport! To Jonah's surprise and regret, Nineveh repents. Jonah's regret reveals a very nasty streak in our human nature which religion can nurture, a tendency to rejoice in the misfortunes of others as long as we ourselves are safe. It is almost as though we need enemies and wicked people around us in order to define how good we are; so we relish scandals and rejoice in condemnation, whether it comes from the pulpit or the tabloid press.

God's will is the salvation of all peoples, and God's will is always effective, so God is at work in every human being. If we really believe this, then instead of denouncing and condemning those who disagree with us, we should listen to them carefully. How can we be so sure that we have unique access to the truth? As Canon Max Warren once wrote, "Our first task in approaching another people, another culture, another religion, is to take off our shoes, for the place we are approaching is holy. Else we may find ourselves treading on men's dreams. More serious still, we may forget that God was here before our arrival."

Thought for the day

"Tread softly, for you tread on my dreams." (W B Yeats, *He Wishes for the Cloths of Heaven*)

Prayer

God, in whom all creation exists, deliver us from the prison of our own narrow certainties, so that we can recognise and reverence you at work in every human being.

Amen.

First Thursday in Lent

Too sophisticated to pray?

Est: 4-17; Ps 137:1-3, 7-8; Mt 7:7-12

Jesus said to his disciples: "Ask, and it will be given to you, search, and you will find; knock, and the door will be opened to you. For the one who asks always receives, the one who searches always finds; the one who knocks will always have the door opened to him."

(Matthew 7:7-8)

We can become very sophisticated about prayer, believing that we have outgrown the need for simple petition. If this is the case, we should be wary of growing up too fast. Dom Chapman's "pray as you can and not as you can't" is excellent advice.

In prayer we may want to thank God, to praise, to complain, or to adore, but the underlying attitude in all our prayer should be acknowledgement of our complete dependence. "Blessed are those who know their needs, theirs is the kingdom of God." Those pictures of scraggy nestlings with mouths wide open, waiting for the parents to bring food, is a good image of the attitude which Jesus recommends.

"But my prayers are not answered," we object. The usual answer, "that's because God knows that it wouldn't be good for you," may be true, but it is infuriating.

What do I really want to ask for? What is it that I really desire? Most of us think we want an endless list of things. However, in praying for them, it may begin to dawn on us that most of our wants are incompatible. I want to be truthful and I want to be popular; I want to be slim and fit, but I also like lots of chocolate and hate exercise.

The struggle is not God's will versus mine: the struggle is my will against myself, leading me to the vital question, what do I most desire? If we keep asking God for things, God will inevitably lead us to this question.

There are many layers of desire in us. The most superficial are usually the loudest. When St Augustine reflected on his life, he wrote, "You have created me for yourself, and my heart is restless until it rests in Thee." If we could reach down to our deepest desire, then we would find the will of God, for God's will is that we should live, and live abundantly.

Thought for the day

Before starting to petition God in prayer, first decide what it is you really want.

Prayer

Lord, save me from every form of pomposity and sophistication. Teach me to pray to you honestly, simply and with childlike trust.

Amen.

Reconciliation comes first

Ezk 18:21-28; Ps 129; Mt 5:20-26

"So then, if you are bringing your offering to the altar and there remember that your brother has something against you, leave your offering there before the altar, go and be reconciled with your brother first, and then come back and present your offering."

(Matthew 5:23-24)

If we were to put this teaching of Jesus into practice, the numbers attending church would decline even more rapidly than they already are! For Jesus, however, reconciliation seems to be more important than churchgoing, and must take precedence.

Even when we do regret an offence we have committed against another, we are often unwilling to apologise, either out of pride, or because we are afraid that the apology will be rejected. So we persuade ourselves that the best course is to do nothing. In this gospel passage, and in his other sayings about forgiveness, Jesus makes no qualifications. We are to forgive another not seven times, but seventy times seven times, and we are to beg forgiveness of those whom we have offended, regardless of whether they are willing to forgive.

If we could only know our own hearts, the wrong we have done and the capacity for evil in us, then we would be so overwhelmed by the goodness of God, who is always ready to forgive, that we could never condemn another person. Neither would fear of rejection make us hold back from apologising for an offence. Knowing that God accepts us, that God loves and cherishes us unconditionally, would protect us from the shattering effects of other people's rejection.

It is difficult for us either to forgive or to ask forgiveness of another. When we face up to the difficulty, we may feel that it is not just difficult, but impossible. We have reached the moment of truth. This is the point at which we have to switch from reliance on our own powers of forgiveness and allow the Spirit of God to take over.

God loves both the person we have offended and the person who has offended us. The process is gradual: we may forgive in prayer, only to find that later on we are still very far from real forgiveness in practice. That is why we have to keep forgiving "seventy times seven times".

Thought for the day

If you kept a record of our sins, Lord, who could stand their ground? (Psalm 130)

Prayer

God, help us to know our sinfulness so that we can know the reality of your forgiveness. Knowing your goodness to us, may we show that same forgiveness to those who have offended us.

Amen.

How practical was Jesus?

Dt 29:16-19; Ps 118:1-2, 4-5, 7-8; Mt 5:43-48.

"You have learnt how it was said: You must love your neighbour and hate your enemy. But I say this to you: love your enemies and pray for those who persecute you; in this way you will be children of your Father in heaven, for he causes the sun to rise on the bad as well as the good, and his rain to fall on the honest and the dishonest alike."

(Matthew 5:44-45)

"Love your enemies and pray for those who persecute you." This is the penance, the change of mind and heart, to which we are called, not only during Lent but throughout our lives. The reason given is that this is the way God is, so that if we are to be at one with God, then this is the way we must behave towards our enemies.

Is Jesus' teaching from the Sermon on the Mount practical? What would the world be like if individuals and nations began to love and do good to their enemies, turned the other cheek, gave their tunic as well as their cloak, if the greatest and most powerful became the servants of all?

If Jesus' teaching is impractical, then we should be honest and say so. If we think that it is a noble ideal for individuals to strive for, but quite useless in public life, then we should say so.

Instead, we dodge the conflict by sealing off Christ's words, reserving them for religious occasions, and we get on with life as usual, competing with one another both as individuals and nations. Pondering the Sermon on the Mount helps us to see the gulf there is between our words and actions. We have internalised our religion so as not to be embarrassed by it in our national and international dealings.

Jesus' teaching is very practical, if we had the courage to accept it. It is at first sight extraordinary that in this century the most outstanding example of a leader who put this teaching into practice was a Hindu, Mahatma Gandhi. On reflection, this should not surprise us, for God is at work in every individual, Christian or non-Christian.

Thought for the day

"The earth has enough for everyone's need but not everyone's greed." (Mahatma Gandhi)

Prayer

God, rid us of our hypocrisy. Give us the courage to face up to and accept your teaching regarding love of our enemies, and let us know the freedom and joy that comes when we put this teaching into practice.

Amen.

Annabel Shilson-Thomas
Second week of Lent

Second Sunday of Lent

Whose sacrifice?

Gn 22:1-2, 9-13, 15-18; Ps 115:10, 15-19; Rm 8:31-34; Mk 9:2-10

God put Abraham to the test. "Abraham, Abraham" he called. "Here I am," he replied. "Take your son," God said, "your only child Isaac, whom you love, and go to the land of Moriah. There you shall offer him as a burnt offering, on a mountain I will point out to you."

(Genesis 22:1-2)

For children, the idea that Abraham could even think of sacrificing Isaac can be terrifying. It's hard to understand a God who demands sacrifice, or to grasp the notion that Abraham's actions were in any way sacrificial. Perhaps as adults we are better placed to realise the tremendous sacrifice Abraham was being asked to make and what it must have cost him to contemplate carrying it through.

The changing face of Israelite history constantly challenged and moulded the Old Testament perception of God – and of sacrifice. A thousand years after Abraham, we hear Amos and his contemporaries promoting justice and righteousness above ritual sacrifice – a strand of prophetic tradition that Jesus develops. Justice for the poor and oppressed is at the heart of his message. Those on the margins of society, including women and children, are given a new value. Their feelings matter.

Yet, as we approach the third millennium, some two thousand years after Christ spoke the immortal words "Suffer little children to come unto me", many parents still face the demand to "sacrifice" their children in order to survive. Today's victims can be found in the sweat shops of Malaysia where children as young as four risk their lives working the heavy machinery that bring us cheap goods; in the sewers of Brazil where children are at the mercy of "clean-up" squads; in the make-shift armies of Africa's forgotten wars where child soldiers learn to kill; and in the brothels of Thailand where child prostitutes satisfy the desire of foreign tourists.

And where, we may ask, is God in all of this? In the agonised sobs of the mother who lets go of her child, in the hollow eyes of the father who cannot afford to raise his family and in the terrified cries of the child who is exploited. Begging that we listen to the voice of Christ from the shadows, from the murky world that we try and ignore but which we are charged with transfiguring.

As the year 2000 approaches, can we raise our voices above the cries of suffering to demand justice? Can we emerge from the darkness we have helped to create and usher in God's kingdom, where all are valued and where all rediscover a child-like innocence? Only then will the fear of shadows cease and the light of Christ's resurrection dawn – for all.

Thought for the day

"*To love God with all your heart and with all your understanding and with all your strength* and *to love your neighbour as yourself* is much more than all the burnt offerings and sacrifices." And when Jesus saw that the scribe answered wisely, he said to him, "You are not far from the kingdom of God." (Mark 12:33-34)

Prayer

Crucified Lord, you sacrificed yourself that others may live. Let your love so burn within us that we too are fired up with the flames of your justice to go forth and transfigure the world.

Amen.

Second Monday of Lent

Different lives

Dn 9:4-10; Ps 78:8-9, 11, 13; Lk 6:36-38

Jesus said to his disciples: "Be compassionate as your Father is compassionate. Do not judge, and you will not be judged yourselves; do not condemn, and you will not be condemned yourselves; grant pardon, and you will be pardoned."

(Luke 6:36-37)

How easy it is to sit in judgement on people, condemning them – and ourselves – in the process. All of us make judgements, consciously and unconsciously, every day of our lives. We judge the man at the bus stop by the newspaper he is reading. We pass the alcoholic slumped outside the shop doorway and feel a sense of distaste. We watch an overwrought mother battle with her wilful child and feel we could handle the situation better.

Such judgements, considered or not, inform the way we relate to people and the relationships we make. How often do we make friends with people whose lives are very different from our own? If this is true of the people we encounter every day, how much more is it true of people whose lives hardly touch us at all, namely, the poor of the developing world?

Do we secretly judge those families who live in degradation amongst the rubbish tips of Manila; the mother who struggles to bring up her children on the streets of Calcutta; the migrant worker who cannot provide for his ever-increasing family; the prostitute who sells her body to feed her husband dying of AIDS? What about the penniless refugee family living next door?

Is not our judgement formed from a position of ignorance which frequently leads to prejudice and condemnation? And does not our condemnation stem from fear because such people remind us of our own vulnerability and mortality?

Can we not use this Lent – a time when we remember our human frailty – as an opportunity to recognise our fear of "poverty" and transform our distaste into compassion? Only when we begin to accept our own poverty will we begin to feel the poverty of others, and be able to stand alongside the poor, rather than stand in judgement over them.

As Christ's Passion teaches us, compassion means sharing the suffering of others, actively responding to their plight and recognising that they too have something to offer us. Christ did not condemn the woman who anointed him with costly oil. He needed her compassion and foretold that her gesture of solidarity would never be forgotten.

We are indebted to each other. We need to recognise that we too stand in need of compassion, otherwise the compassion that we exercise ourselves may become simply patronising – something the poor can do without.

Thought for the day

Condemnation is a quick cure for fear, whereas compassion is a slow-burning response to suffering. It demands of us that we accompany people to places from which we would rather flee.

Prayer

Compassionate God, give us the courage to share the suffering of others that together we may rise up and know the power of resurrection.

Amen.

Second Tuesday of Lent

Practise what you preach

Is 1:10, 16-20; Ps 49:8-9, 16-17, 21, 23; Mt 23:1-2

Addressing the people and his disciples Jesus said, "The scribes and the Pharisees occupy the chair of Moses. You must therefore do what they tell you and listen to what they say; but do not be guided by what they do, since they do not practise what they preach."

(Matthew 23:1-3)

"Power corrupts. Absolute power corrupts absolutely." There is much truth in this saying. How many of us can handle the responsibility that power carries? The scribes and the Pharisees, the keepers of the law of Moses, failed miserably. Many of our own politicians fall short of the standards they claim to uphold, even church leaders are not always exempt from the charge of hypocrisy. Should we dare to take a good, hard look at ourselves – something we are asked to do each Lent – we will see that we also fail sometimes to "practise what we preach".

Jesus was acutely aware of how power could be abused. Throughout his ministry, he grappled with the question of what kind of messiah he was to be; a messiah who would pander to popular belief, jumping from the top of the temple to prove his divinity, or a messiah who would assume the role of the suffering servant of Isaiah. Jesus chose the latter and asks us to do the same. He asks us to turn the world's view of power on its head, so that strength is found in weakness, riches in poverty.

How hard this is, and how easy it is for us to lose sight of what the Christian life is about. All too frequently we become slaves to ourselves, chaining ourselves to our own egos, becoming trapped in the enclosed world of self-delusion. On occasion we blindly follow others, failing to see that they too are ensnared in the deluded world of self-promotion. Even church groups can flounder and disintegrate if they are allowed to become battle grounds for personalities to work out their own agendas!

Perhaps one of the questions we should ask ourselves as we approach the millennium is, what motivates us? Are we servants of the Gospel? Do we listen to our brothers and sisters in the developing world, or do we arrogantly set their development agenda, forgetting that "all who humble themselves will be exalted, but all who exalt themselves will be humbled".

Let us use the run-up to the millennium to work out what Jesus' topsy-turvy maxim really means, and how we can apply it in our lives. Then perhaps we will be able to enter the new millennium with integrity, as people who have learned to practise what we preach.

Thought for the day

Where does our power lie? Do we use it responsibly as servants of the Gospel?

Prayer

Christ, our Servant King, open our hearts that we may embrace your Gospel, finding strength in weakness and riches in poverty.

Amen.

Second Wednesday of Lent

Praying from the edge

Jr 18:18-20; Ps 30:5-6, 14-16; Mt 20:17-28

Listen to me Lord,
hear what my adversaries are saying.
Should evil be returned for good?
For they are digging a pit for me.
Remember how I stood in your presence
to plead on their behalf,
to turn your wrath away from them.

(Jeremiah 18:19-20)

Of all the Old Testament prophets, Jeremiah is probably the most human, the one who wears his heart on his sleeve, who feels the attacks against him most acutely, and who is most forthcoming in telling God exactly how he feels. There is no beating about the bush with Jeremiah! Disarming honesty is his trademark, the kind of honesty that is characteristic of the poor, who have nothing to hide and nothing to lose – save the courage to speak out. Such honesty is unnerving. It exposes our sophisticated "cover-up" techniques and challenges our security.

How many of us are able to admit to our vulnerability, or openly to acknowledge our pain and hurt when those we have loved and trusted betray us? Yet we expect the poor to live with such vulnerability day in day out. They have no choice but to expose themselves to the danger and hurt of betrayal – for they have nothing to protect them.

I wonder how we would react to such insecurity; to the daily possibility of losing our wage for failing to reach impossible targets set by our employer; to the knowledge that any day we could be forced off the land where we are managing to eke out a living; to a life overshadowed by the threat of violence because we are unable to repay a long-standing family debt?

Would we not cry out in protest? Would we not demand some kind of explanation from God? And would God not understand our sense of injustice and betrayal; the God who was betrayed by one of the twelve closest to him; the God who was denied three times by his best friend, Peter; who was crucified by the world he came to save?

This Lent, let us learn from the honesty of the poor. Let us acknowledge our own "poverty" and approach God with the characteristic vulnerability of those who live on the edge. Let us take courage from their champion, Jeremiah, and be open to the truth, so that the prayers we utter not only bring us into a closer relationship with our maker, but with our fellow human beings. Then perhaps, with our neighbours in the developing world, we can move towards the millennium with greater vision and a renewed sense of the possibility of transformation for all.

Thought for the day

Does our natural desire for self-protection interfere with our relationship with God? Does it make us less sensitive to the needs of our neighbour?

Prayer

Vulnerable God, give us the courage to be open to ourselves and to others; that we may find you in the hidden places of our world so that our darkness is turned to light.

Amen.

Second Thursday of Lent

Changing the ending

Jr 17:5-10; Ps 1:1-4, 6; Lk 16:19-31

"In his torment in Hades the rich man looked up and saw Abraham a long way off with Lazarus in his bosom. So he cried out, 'Father Abraham, pity me and send Lazarus to dip the tip of his finger in water and cool my tongue, for I am in agony in these flames.'"

(Luke 16:23-24)

This story of the rich man and Lazarus is deliberately hard-hitting. It is designed to evoke a response and gives no room for manoeuvre. Jesus must have left little doubt in the minds of the Pharisees as to what he was driving at: their hardness of heart would not go unpunished. Either they must face up to the reality of their behaviour or suffer the consequences.

Even if the pictorial images of heaven and hell may no longer fit in with our world view, we would be foolish to try and escape the message. As the story of the Good Samaritan challenges us to decide whether we are a priest, Levite or Good Samaritan, here too we are challenged to consider what being a good neighbour demands of us.

Whilst we cannot re-write history, we can re-write the ending of the story. The immutable gulf that Abraham speaks of is immutable only if we make it so. For, if we can but see it, the poor, like Christ, offer us the hope of redemption. Our response to their suffering helps our transformation as well as theirs. Had the rich man offered Lazarus even the scraps from his table, the beginnings of a relationship would have been fostered – albeit only a small beginning. Who knows where such a gesture may have taken them? To a place, one would hope, where the humanity of rich and poor alike was affirmed.

Witness South Africa. As Nelson Mandela in particular, has demonstrated the aggrieved black South Africans have readily received the tentative hand of friendship extended by their white oppressors, and the process of rebuilding and transforming that once broken land has begun.

Let us not delude ourselves, however, that changing the story is easy. If our response to the poor is motivated purely by self-interest, we remain like the rich man, trapped in a world of make-believe which we are incapable of transforming by ourselves.

If the story's ending is to change, the rich first need to acknowledge their part in generating the world's suffering and cry out for Lazarus' forgiveness. For then, and only then, will the bridge between rich and poor begin to be built. And only then will the process of transforming the landscape on either side begin.

Thought for the day

Do we recognise Christ in the people we meet?

Prayer

O Christ, you bear the wounds of suffering humanity. Forgive us for the times we have watched you suffer and passed by on the other side. Help us to reach out to take your hand, so that together we may build the bridge that leads to your kingdom.

Amen.

Second Friday of Lent

Passing the buck

Gn 37:3-4, 12-13, 17-28; Ps 104:16-21; Mt 21:33-43, 45-46

Looking up they saw a group of Ishmaelites who were coming from Gilead, their camels laden with gum, tragacanth, balsam and resin, which they were taking down into Egypt. Then Judah said to his brothers, "What do you gain by killing our brother and covering up his blood? Come let us sell him to the Ishmaelites, but let us not do any harm to him. After all he is our brother, and our own flesh." His brothers agreed.

(Genesis 37:25-27)

The story of Joseph, exciting as it is, hardly flatters human nature. It tells of jealousy, violence, betrayal and greed. It also reveals a willingness on the part of Joseph's brothers to evade responsibility for their actions. Their mutual complicity in their decision to sell Joseph protects them, as does their transaction with a third party, the Ishmaelites. Responsibility is so dissipated that they even delude themselves they are doing their brother a favour by not killing him – "after all he is our brother, and our own flesh."

I wonder how often we convince ourselves that the responsibility for something is not ours. In a world where decision-making is increasingly global and out of our hands it is easy – and convenient – to pass the buck. Feeling impotent is not without its compensations, especially when it makes our lives easier and reinforces the view that we are not accountable to others.

In a global economy it is difficult to know exactly where to point the finger of blame. Who, for example, is responsible for the slave-like working conditions of Bangladeshi women and children locked in textile factories for up to 16 hours a day, or the one million children in servitude to the carpet industries of India, Pakistan and Nepal? Is it the factory owner, the multi-national company that the factory supplies, the giant transnational corporations that operate all over the world, or the consumer, you and I, for buying a product where each thread has been knotted with the childhood of a young boy or girl?

In whatever way we decide to apportion blame, we cannot escape responsibility for our part in the world's inhumanity. We cannot pass the buck. Our Christian faith demands that we fight injustice; demands, for example, that we campaign for the cancellation of Third World debt which perpetuates the manufacture of cheap goods made for our consumption by the blood and sweat of the poor. To turn a blind-eye is to collude with a system which dehumanises us all. The people of the Third World are our brothers and sisters. Even Joseph's brothers – albeit reluctantly – recognised some responsibility towards their own flesh and blood. How much more should we?

Thought for the day

"No man is an island, entire of itself. Every man is a piece of the continent, a part of the main ... Any man's death diminishes me, because I am involved in mankind."
(John Donne)

Prayer

Lord, you have no ears but ours to hear the cries of those who suffer, no eyes but ours to see their face, no feet but ours to tread your path, no hands but ours to do your work; use us in your service, that others may feel your touch and be healed.

Amen.

Second Saturday of Lent

The price of forgiving

Mi 7:14-15, 18-20; Ps 102:1-4, 9-12; Lk 15:1-3, 11-32

"While he was still a long way off, his father saw him and was moved with pity. He ran to the boy and clasped him in his arms and kissed him tenderly."

(Luke 15:20)

The parable of the prodigal son gives us insight into the true nature of forgiveness. It speaks to us of compassion and generosity; the kind of compassion and generosity that is revealed in the cross, the supreme symbol of sacrificial love.

Despite the power of forgiveness, we frequently forget the enormity of its cost. Thank God the older brother in the parable is there to remind us just how difficult true forgiveness is; that it is not based on things being fair or equal, but springs from a love that is prepared to cross boundaries and embrace the offender, offering the hope of resurrection.

If we stop for a moment and acknowledge what a problem truly forgiving someone presents for us, perhaps we will begin to see the enormity of what we are asking of our neighbours in the Third World. Think what it must cost Vincenta, whose husband was one of 40,000 Mayan Indians murdered by Guatemala's military death squads in the early 1980s. Think what it must cost Katan, landmine victim and double amputee of Cambodia's civil war. Think what it must cost Shila, kidnapped from Nepal and sold into an Indian brothel at the age of eleven.

How can Vincenta, Katan and Shila possibly begin to forgive the perpetrators of such crimes? And how can they possibly forgive us, for we are part of the world that sat back and silently watched their suffering.

That world continues to sit back impassively as the policies of the World Bank and the IMF make it hard for people like Vincenta to rebuild their shattered lives and make a living. Western governments cannot even agree to a global ban on landmines; meanwhile in the developing world hunger is forcing parents to sell their children into prostitution.

But the poor and oppressed refuse to be our victims. All too frequently it is they who show us the power of resurrection, they who live life despite the odds, they who show us the meaning of solidarity and partnership in the face of inequality and oppression – and they who show us what true forgiveness means. For they are the crucified people of today, who reach out from their cross to offer us the hope of new life. Are we not indebted to them?

Thought for the day

"Is it nothing to you, all you that pass by?" (John Stainer, *The Crucifixion*)

Prayer

Crucified Lord, forgive us for the times we have remained inert in the face of suffering. Grant us the grace to receive forgiveness from those who show us the power of your resurrection.

Amen.

Peter Selby
Third week of Lent

Third Sunday of Lent

God's new way to freedom

Ex 20:1-17; Ps 18:8-11; 1 Co 1:22-25; Jn 2:13-25

God's foolishness is wiser than human wisdom, and God's weakness is stronger than human strength.

(1 Corinthians 1:25)

South Africa today is a nation designing itself from scratch. The people and their leaders have to decide what it is to be a country, what are to be its guiding principles and how they will be put into effect. The same must be true of those countries reconstituting themselves after long decades of communist rule.

In such places the past seems to contain no models, and yet traumatic as the past was, it seemed to contain a certain security, and it is hard to get used to having that taken away. A new way of being a nation has to be invented, and that requires imagination and patience.

The verses we call "The Ten Commandments", the law God gave to his people on Sinai, are just such a social code for a new people. It condemns the oppressive ways of the past, which God, having brought them from slavery, requires them to avoid. The wanderings in the wilderness were a time for trying to find that new way of being a nation, but the people often lamented the loss of the security of the past, easily forgetting how oppressive it had been. God's call to be a new kind of nation seemed hard to understand, let alone to fulfil.

Likewise, St Paul's commendation of the way of the crucified seemed foolishness even to those who had experienced life on the margins of society. In comparison to Christ's way, the traditional exercise of power, expertise and status seemed secure, and therefore attractive.

Slavery is not the thing of the past we might wish, and all nations need huge gifts of imagination if they are to express God's way of justice in today's world. When Our Lord confronted the exclusion of the nations from the Temple by traders, he presented us with a sign of God's new way of inclusive love: something that can seem like foolishness and weakness to us as we seek a regulated and ordered society.

We cannot conceive of a national life that is not regulated by status and the power of money, even if those things leave many excluded from our common life. But is not Christ's way in fact God's new way to freedom, for people and nations?

Thought for the day

There are some kinds of slavery which are forced on people who have no choice; but there are others which people choose, because they cannot bear the uncertainty and newness of following Christ's way.

Prayer

Heavenly Father, guide and bless all nations who face the challenge of making a new beginning. Protect us all from being bound to ways of thinking and acting which hold us back from following in your way of generous love. May we know that what we often see as the weakness of love is in fact your strength. Through our strong and gentle Saviour, Jesus Christ.

Amen.

Third Monday of Lent

Unbounded mercy

1 K 5:1-15; Pss 41:2-3; 42:3-4; Lk 4:24-30

"There were many widows in Israel, I can assure you, in Elijah's day, when heaven remained shut for three years and six months and a great famine raged throughout the land, but Elijah was not sent to any one of these: he was sent to a widow at Zarephath, a Sidonian town."

(Luke 4:25-26)

What are we to make of all the indignation in today's readings? First, Naaman is enraged that a person of his importance is turned away from Elisha's house by a mere messenger with an inexplicable order. Then the congregation at Nazareth is furious with an upstart from their own village who tells them the hard truth that prophesying to your own people often falls on deaf ears, giving two examples of how God's generosity ignores national and ethnic boundaries.

The first thing that strikes us is how utterly human this indignation is, how it accords with our life experience and often our own inner feelings too. If you seek to organise a class in school, the pay structure in a company department, or even your own family without taking into account our tendency to self-importance and our convictions about our rights, you will be doomed to failure.

This is even more apparent in political questions. Whether you are looking for a site for travellers or discussing immigration policies, you will surely come up against your own and others' conviction that boundaries are to be safeguarded: the stranger is regarded not as a possible bringer of new insights and gifts, but as one likely to endanger our own position.

We all know that religious belief does not make us immune to these human tendencies; indeed it often accentuates them to the point where we believe that God is on the side of "us" against "them". So if we see ourselves in the indignation of a Naaman or of the congregation at Nazareth, how do we interpret God's will for humankind? Is our concern to defend ourselves, our standing and our national boundaries all bad?

When a tendency is so deep in the human heart, we shouldn't damn it absolutely. For the need to know where we are is part of our natural desire for some security. What Christ seeks for us, however, is an opening-out of our hearts, a willingness to acknowledge God in the stranger and to accept that those who are different, from outside our group, belong to us, because like us they belong to God.

We often find each other an intrusion and a threat; God teaches us that we also represent for each other potential sources of grace and new life.

Thought for the day

Are there ways in which I should be working for a more inclusive community? And a more inclusive heart?

Prayer

Give me grace, O God of love, to see your Son's arms wide open on the Cross. May I truly desire his gift of a heart so thankful for your mercy to me, that I do not begrudge your gifts in others.

Amen.

Third Tuesday of Lent

Forgiveness, God's policy

Dn 3:25, 34-43; Ps 24:4-9; Mt 18:21-35

"I cancelled all that debt of yours when you appealed to me. Were you not bound, then, to have pity on your fellow servant just as I had pity on you?"

(Matthew 18:32-33)

We know that it is possible for people to take the Bible too literally, and in the process to neglect its deeper meaning. But we can also lose sight of its meaning by not taking it literally enough.

The "debt" of which the gospel parable speaks can refer to our relationships with God and each other; but Our Lord is also speaking directly of a problem his hearers – and many of us – know only too well: the frightening reality of debts that cannot be repaid.

We are becoming increasingly aware of the desperate plight of developing nations who can never hope to repay their enormous debts; as a wealthy nation we need to help lift their burdens and ensure that those nations are not forced into such debts again.

We also to need remember those in our own country who find it impossible to avoid getting into the trap of serious debt from which there is no escape. Anyone in such a situation needs our prayers and our support to form a society where such traps are not set for the most vulnerable, and where those who have money are not tempted into constant greed for more.

The man in the parable who was let off a large debt failed to understand that this forgiveness was not a one-off; it was real policy change, which he too was expected to adopt. In God's kingdom we should not relate to one another as creditor and debtor but as brother and sister.

That requires not just new economics, but a real change of heart. We may want a policy of forgiveness only when it suits us, ignoring those whose need for it is much greater than ours. The fact is that our society is becoming more and more money-driven, as demonstrated by the ever-expanding column inches in the newspapers which tell us how to spend our money and ignore those who are struggling to survive financially.

Out of the change of heart that we will need to bring about a world of economic justice will come changes in other aspects of how we relate to each other. Any tendency to meanness will be challenged by God's constant forgiveness, and our tendency to notice what others owe us (in every sense) will be softened by an awareness of the mercy we have received and upon which we depend.

Thought for the day

One of the biggest mountains faith needs to move is the mountain of debt.

Prayer

Remember your mercy, Lord, and the love you have shown from of old. Soften my heart and the hearts of us all when we fail to be merciful, and forget what we have been forgiven; through Jesus Christ our Lord.

Amen.

Third Wednesday of Lent

The wisdom of obedience

Dt 4:1, 5-9; Ps 147:12-13, 15-16, 19-20; Mt 5:17-19

"Do not forget the things your eyes have seen, nor let them slip from your heart all the days of your life; rather, tell them to your children and to your children's children."

(Deuteronomy 4:9)

What is the secret of the good life, for a person and for a nation? What does wisdom consist of for those who wish to direct their own lives rightly, or who have the responsibility of authority in society or in the Church?

The book of Deuteronomy functioned as the great charter of reform and renewal in the seventh century before Christ. It takes the form of a great speech delivered in the wilderness by Moses, God's chosen leader of Israel in the days of the exodus from Egypt.

It recalls Israel to the way of life and values they had been taught and which, in the settled life of the Promised Land, they had often forsaken. It contains much detailed guidance for the regulation of their society, for the God of Israel was concerned with the precision of justice and law.

Above all, however, Deuteronomy is a reminder of an ancient experience, of the covenant which God had made with his people, recalling a lost vision of what it meant to be God's people. It therefore convicts the Israelites primarily of forgetfulness, of a reluctance to remember their calling and the demands God had made of them. In presenting its call to reform and renewal in this way, the book of Deuteronomy reminds us – as it reminded its original hearers – of the importance of remembering and obeying to a well-ordered, successful society.

As the Church, we are guardians of that life-giving remembrance; in the stories we tell and in our celebration of the Eucharist. We gather together, amongst other things, to be recalled to our central purpose, to the primary vision God gave us to cherish and to share. As the gospel reading makes clear, following Jesus is no less demanding than following the law of Moses; he came to affirm, not to cancel.

Cherishing the vision we have been given and sharing it "with our children and our children's children", in word and action, in prayer and living, is not something we do just for our own spiritual health. We also believe it is the truest wisdom for our communities, our nations and our world. Like Israel of old, we believe in a society whose law and pattern of life reflects God's commands. We are constantly in need of being recalled to that vision.

Thought for the day

The sacred memory of what God has done recalls and renews us.

Prayer

By your spirit heal us, O God of truth, of all forgetfulness of what you have done for us and the life to which you have called us in your Son, Jesus Christ.

Amen.

Third Thursday of Lent

The undivided kingdom

Jr 7:23-28; Ps 94:1-2, 6-9; Lk 11:14-23

Jesus said "Every kingdom divided against itself is heading for ruin, and a household divided against itself collapses."

(Luke 11:17)

We need very few lessons in the modern world about the power of division to harm the best causes and destroy time and time again every opportunity of change for the better, (fortunately, Satan is equally vulnerable to division, as this reading says). How many struggles for liberation have foundered when those who should be working together end up at loggerheads.

On this Thursday, as we recall Our Lord's prayer "that they may all be one", we remember in particular the damage done to the cause of Christ by the disunity of Christians. We give thanks for all that has been achieved, not least in our own century, in breaking down suspicion between Christians and enabling a degree of common prayer and service that not so long ago seemed impossible.

As we remind ourselves of just how much Christ's cause suffers when we are divided, we pray for grace to enter into ever deeper unity, learning to be enriched by what we receive from others.

We should remember that our disunity damages not simply the Church, as though it existed for itself, but the mission to the world for which it exists. We lament disunity and pray for unity so that the world may believe and discover the truth to which all are called, a truth which summons us all into harmony with each other.

The night of Christ's prayer for the unity of his people is also the night when we remember one of the most searing aspects of his Passion, the betrayal. Disunity amongst those who need to work closely together always has a sharp sense of betrayal about it, which is why some of the quarrels between Christians have been so passionate, even violent. That sense of betrayal comes through in the pain in God's address to his people through the prophet: "They refused to face me and turned their backs on me."

At the same time, we give thanks that out of that betrayal God has once more given us the possibility of becoming an undivided kingdom, united in faith and hope and love, a kingdom which will not fail in its purposes because it is no longer divided against itself.

Thought for the day

If the power of division can be lethal, how great can be the power of unity.

Prayer

As grain once scattered in the fields and grapes once dispersed on the hillsides are united on the altar in bread and wine, so may your Church be gathered from the ends of the earth into the peace and unity of your Kingdom. Even so, come Lord Jesus.

Amen.

Third Friday of Lent

The promise of new beginning

Ho 14:2-10; Ps 80:6, 8-11, 14, 17; Mk 12:28-34

I will heal their disloyalty,
I will love them with all my heart,
for my anger has turned from them.
I will fall like dew on Israel.
He shall bloom like the lily,
and thrust out roots like the poplar.

(Hosea 14:4-5)

The forty days of Lent symbolise Our Lord's forty days in the desert, which in turn were a re-enactment of the forty years the Israelites spent in the wilderness. For Jesus as for the Israelites, these were long and testing periods, when faith in God's promise was put to the test. The days of Lent, therefore, are days of self-examination and refreshment, when we remind ourselves of God's promise of a new beginning, in preparation for Holy Week and Easter.

That promise of God is above all a promise of his continuing love – whatever the world may do. God's pledge, here recounted by Hosea, to love us with all his heart, is reiterated in Our Lord's summary of the first commandment: "You shall love the Lord your God with all your heart". We love because God first loved us – and has promised to love us to the end. His love is as refreshing as dew on a thirsty land, reviving a people whose loyalty has faltered.

The prophet speaks of "disloyalty" because he knows that God has competitors in the lives of his people: other gods and idols whose ways they prefer. That begs the question, who or what are the idols of our society (for idols were not chosen by individuals but were what the nation was tempted to worship)?

Earlier this week we reflected on the power of one such idol in the life of our society, that of money (to which Our Lord gives a divine name, Mammon).

We trust in money, we believe we cannot do without it, we think it holds the solution to most of our personal and social problems. In reality, however, that solution lies in loyalty to the Lord's command to love him and our neighbour as ourselves – it is from loyal obedience to that way that our well-being as individuals and as a society comes.

We are called upon as a society, therefore, to consider again where we have misplaced our trust, where we have wrongly looked for solutions and for salvation. The promise of a new beginning comes when we recognise that although our loyalty and commitment may falter, God's never will, as we shall see on Good Friday in the steadfast obedience which led Christ not to flee from the cross.

Thought for the day

Trust is found only in God, in holding to him as he has held to us.

Prayer

O God, whose most dear Son went not up to joy before he suffered pain, and entered not into glory before he was crucified, grant that we, walking in the way of the cross, may find it none other than the way of life and peace.

Amen.

Third Saturday of Lent

True humility

Ho 5:15-6:6; Ps 50:3-4, 18-21; Lk 18:9-14

"All who humble themselves will be exalted, but all who exalt themselves will be humbled."

(Luke 18:14)

Among the besetting difficulties of religious people is the tendency to demonstrate their devotion by the ways in which they differ from other people. Was the prayer of the Pharisee in the parable really so exceptionally arrogant? Aren't we exalting ourselves in the same way when we dismiss the Pharisees as appallingly smug and self-righteous – so unlike ourselves!

The Pharisee's prayer reflects his sincere gratitude that he has been enabled to live a life different from others. By giving thanks for this, he follows that most dangerous of human instincts – to set ourselves apart from, and above, our fellow beings.

In contrast, the publican's prayer places him right in the midst of the human condition, a member of the class of "sinner". He shares the lot of those human beings who, precisely because they cannot achieve a manner of life that sets them apart, become the despised of society and are forcibly relegated to its margins.

It is principally to these people that Christ comes, offering a righteousness they cannot achieve for themselves. Those who do not set themselves apart for their virtuous behaviour are the ones who receive the reward for it: those who humble themselves will be exalted.

The parable also portrays Christ's own chosen position on the edge of society, in the company of sinners. Saturday is the day for remembering Christ lying in the tomb, the pre-eminent example of him sharing our lot. We acknowledge the fact that he allowed himself to be humbled, "they made his grave with the wicked" (Isaiah 53:9), and we await the good news of his exaltation.

In all of this we see a clear picture of the Christian life: we are most likely to be faithful, most clearly living in the image of Christ, when we do not set ourselves apart from others, but instead place ourselves in solidarity with our fellow human beings. The greatest of the saints have been those who were willing to share the lot of humanity, and in particular that section of humanity whom society seeks to cast out.

Thought for the day

I cannot place myself beyond God's reach, unless I seek to be beyond the reach of my sisters and brothers.

Prayer

Father, as your Son lay in the tomb and so shared our mortality, so may we be willing to share in the lives of our sisters and brothers in humility and love.

Amen.

Karl Gaspar
Fourth week of Lent

Fourth Sunday of Lent

Rage against the dying of the light

2 Ch 36:14-16, 19-23; Ps 136; Ep 2:4-10; Jn 3:14-21

On these grounds is sentence pronounced:
that though the light has come into the world
people have shown they prefer
darkness to the light
because their deeds were evil.

(John 3:19)

In the Philippines, there is a folk saying which goes: those who refuse to look back at their past will not reach their destination. History is an integral part of how people see their destiny.

Writing about the eighteenth and nineteenth century British trade with Asia, Fr John Schumacher SJ observed: "In order to have goods to barter for Chinese tea, the British traded firearms to Sulu in exchange for its sea and forest products. These labor-intensive products in turn needed a large number of slaves to gather them."

This trade reality persists today, despite the demise of colonialism. There are, of course, differences in the way trade is conducted, in the current mad rush towards globalisation. But western countries, still consuming vast quantities of Asian goods, still largely ignore the slave-like working conditions imposed on many local labourers – including children.

In addition, the deepest coral reefs and the highest mountains – the source of many traded goods – are suffering a process of disintegration that will ultimately render hundreds of species of flora and fauna extinct. In human terms, the impact of this ecological damage is being felt most keenly by the poor.

Close to two millennia ago, light came into the world when the Son of Man was crucified and resurrected. This event manifested God's great love for us.

Despite this light, however, many of us would rather remain in the shadows. Cheap consumer goods are so convenient that we hesitate to protest against unfair trade practices that hurt the economies of poor countries. Our comfortable lifestyles encourage us to ignore the ecological disasters which threaten our world.

We should rage against the dying of the light, and walk forwards into the light. Both for our own sakes and for the future of the world, we need to perform light-sharing and life-giving acts that celebrate creation rather than damaging it, acts that truly enrich the lives of all, not just a few.

In return for all God's blessings, especially the light that came with Jesus, the least we can do is to open a window, so that the darkness around us will be flooded with colour. Such is the landscape of the promised reign of God, which is ours if we take each other's hands, and face our destiny as children of light.

Thought for the day

"But you are a chosen race, a kingdom of priests, a holy nation, God's own people, chosen to proclaim the wonderful acts of God, who called you out of darkness into his own marvellous light." (1 Peter 2:9)

Prayer

Lord, it is so easy to remain lost in darkness and so difficult to step forward into the light – it demands a real change in our priorities. Help us to tap into the wellsprings of our hearts and the energy in the depths of our being, to move us to celebrate creation and build communities among the peoples of the world.

Amen.

Fourth Monday of Lent

Let the children live

Is 65:17-21; Ps 29:2, 4-6, 11-13; Jn 4:43-54

Now there was a court official there whose son was ill at Capernaum and, hearing that Jesus had arrived in Galilee from Judaea, he went and asked him to come and cure his son as he was at the point of death ... "Go home," said Jesus, "your son will live."

(John 4: 46-50)

In July 1996, *Time* magazine reported a happy reunion between a father and his two sons in Manyiel in southern Sudan. Seven years earlier, Akok Deng Kuot and his half-brother Garang had been captured by a slave trader during a raid on their village. At the time they were respectively seven and five years old.

The two boys were taken to the north where they were forced to work on farms, fetching and carrying, and sweeping cow dung. They were fed sour milk and table scraps and locked up at night.

Two American journalists from the *Baltimore Sun* tracked down the slave trader. They succeeded in buying the boys back and reunited them with their overjoyed father. This transaction highlighted the trade in human beings, particularly children, which despite government denials is reportedly common in the Sudan.

In defiance of the United Nations Convention on the Rights of the Child, children are suffering from a lack of freedom all over the world. There is child slavery in factories, in marketplaces and on farms. Sarah Balabagan, a 14-year-old from southern Philippines, highlighted the plight of young girls working as domestic helpers in the Middle East, when she hit the headlines for stabbing the employer in Saudi Arabia who had attempted to rape her.

The children of the world are the future of the world; their enslavement ties the world in chains. If nothing is done to transform the world economy which continues to make the rich world richer and the poor world poorer, then the end result will be that more children will suffer.

Suffer not the children. Like the official that Jesus met in Cana, our hearts should be with our children who are in need. Believing in Jesus, the official sought his assistance, and sure enough, Christ's intervention saved the child. Like Jesus, we too must intervene on behalf of children who are suffering. The children need us. But because they show us the way to the kingdom, we need the children more.

Thought for the day

"Think of the children in slavery and help to free them from the storm,
For it is our joint responsibility to keep them safe, to keep them warm."
(The Carpenters, *Bless the Beasts and the Children*)

Prayer

We pray for children experiencing the slavery that Garang and Akok Deng Kuot and Sarah Balabagan suffered in their young lives; may they too be safely returned to their families. Lord, help us to do our share in building a bright future for the children of the world.

Amen.

Fourth Tuesday of Lent

Stream of living water

Ezk 47:1-9, 12; Ps 45:2-3, 5-6, 8-9; Jn 5:1-3, 5-16

"Wherever the river flows, all living creatures teeming in it will live ... Along the river on either bank, will grow every kind of fruit tree with leaves that never wither and fruit that never fails; they will bear new fruit every month because this water comes from the sanctuary. And their fruit will be good to eat and the leaves medicinal."

(Ezekiel 47:6-9, 12)

"How much is a river worth? Too often, with the prevalence of a deeply ingrained 'profit-ethic' in modern society, everything is considered as being up for sale. Sadly, Creation and even human rights have been included."

This was the poignant lament of Federico Jose Lagdameo of NASSA, the Filipino Church's National Secretariat for Social Action, Justice and Peace, after a major ecological tragedy on the island of Marinduque, south of Manila.

In 1969 a Canadian company began mining operations in Marinduque, despite protests led by the local Church, who instantly foresaw grave dangers for the local community.

The highly toxic refuse from the mine was simply dumped into the nearby bay, quickly leading to the destruction of coral reefs and fish sanctuaries, and to a dwindling catch for the fishing community. Protests continued and the company was ordered to devise a less destructive waste disposal system.

A disused open pit was employed instead. But this pit had a drainage tunnel at the bottom leading to the Boac River. The company plugged this tunnel but in March 1996 the plug gave way and for four days tons of mine waste poured into the river.

More than 1,300 people had to be evacuated. The livelihood of thousands more was affected. Close to a million dollars' worth of freshwater and marine life and rich agricultural lands were destroyed. Today, the Boac river is dead.

This is not an isolated story. Countries rushing towards industrialisation need electricity; unfortunately, planners create huge dams despite their negative impact on fluvial eco-systems. Industrial plants are built alongside rivers, with grave results.

In this reading from Ezekiel, the Holy Spirit, as a stream of living water, encourages nature to burst forth. The river comes from the Temple (in other words, from God), and with it come trees and flowers, fish and butterflies.

Whilst this recalls the biblical image of God's healing in a sterile and sinful world, new meanings can be discerned in today's context of the need to protect the environment.

We need to believe in the God of creation whose Spirit is living water. We need to believe that we are called to be co-creators. We have to become rivers; wherever we flow, we should seek to bring abundant life.

Thought for the day

"Nature and all else in God's creation can never be fully weighed in monetary terms. They cannot really be commodified and tagged with a price. They are intangibles in the realm of what is truly valuable." (Federico Jose Lagdameo)

Prayer

Spirit of God in the clear running waters, wash away our indifference to acts that damage your natural world. Empower us to break through our fears and disappointments so that in solidarity with our brothers and sisters in this global village, we can protect and nurture creation.

Amen.

Fourth Wednesday of Lent

Look up to the mountains!

Is 49:8-15; Ps 144:8-9, 13-14, 17-18; Jn 5:17-30

Shout for joy, you heaven; exult you earth!
You mountains, break into happy cries!
For the Lord consoles his people
and takes pity on those who are afflicted.

(Isaiah 49:13)

Reading about mountains reminds us of those indigenous people who live amongst mountain ranges, worshipping gods of nature. There are an estimated 300 million indigenous people in the world, spread across more than 70 countries. Most consider their ancestral domain in the plains and mountains as their rightful homeland; they continue to hold on to a cosmology where the earth's creator and the spirit-world are part of their day-to-day reality.

The present thrust of aggressive development is threatening their culture with extinction. In the Philippines, for example, mining, logging and tourism projects are crowding onto ancestral lands. Whilst it is easy to feel that we are more "sophisticated" than the indigenous peoples, they are living in much closer communion with nature than we are. If the idea of mountains breaking into happy cries seems hard for us to imagine, then we have much to learn from their experience of living hand in hand with God's creation.

Even so, how can the earth exult when the vulnerable people of the earth have so little protection?

In the world's hierarchy, indigenous people are considered the least of our brothers and sisters, yet they are in the forefront of defending the natural world against industrial interests as they seek to protect their homelands. Caring about our world and its future for our children means feeling compassion for their cause.

God calls on us to take pity on those who are afflicted, particularly during the season of Lent. If we allow God's spirit to move us then we will be able to stand back from our materialism and help to recreate a world where the songs of the earth and the cries of the mountains will once more break forth across the face of our planet.

Thought for the day

"Land is a grace that must be nurtured. To enrich it is the eternal exhortation of Apo Kabunian* to his entire children. Land is sacred. Land is beloved. From its womb springs our Kalinga life." (Macliing Dulag, a Kalinga tribal leader killed by the Marcos military in the Philippines for opposing a dam project that would have submerged his people's homeland.)

* The Kalinga people's name for God.

Prayer

God of earth and mountains, God of our ancestors, hear our plea. Today we pray for those whose lives are most threatened by the damage inflicted on your precious gift to us – creation. For our own sake as well as theirs, give us strength to make the right choices for our planet.

Amen.

Fourth Thursday of Lent

Radical discipleship

Ex 32:7-14; Ps 105:19-23; Jn 5:31-47

Were I to testify on my own behalf,
my testimony would not be valid;
but there is another witness who can speak on my behalf,
and I know that his testimony is valid.

(John 5:31-32)

Jose Antonio Neves is not a name that immediately springs to mind alongside that of Nelson Mandela, Aung San Suu Kyi, Vaclav Havel, Alexander Solzhenitsyn, Ninoy Aquino, Dietrich Bonhoeffer, or John the Baptist. But Jose too was a prisoner of conscience, although only a few people outside of East Timor have heard of him, and like these more familiar names he too is to be admired for his prophetic testimony.

Jose, a student and human rights activist, was arrested in Malang, East Java in May 1994 for sending information to foreign organisations about human rights violations committed by the Indonesian military. He was found guilty and sentenced to four years in prison. Amnesty International classified him as a prisoner of conscience.

There are thousands of Joses languishing in prisons in China, Burma, Turkey, Somalia, Burundi, North Korea and Guatemala, whose plight testifies to their courage and the strength of their convictions. With the collapse of many dictatorships in Latin America and other areas, some countries have fewer political detainees. But torture and imprisonment without trial are still widespread.

The bravery and selflessness of political prisoners can inspire hundreds, even thousands of other people. Their testimony of a life willingly offered for the sake of their nation, the poor or oppressed, for justice and freedom, has empowered others to get involved in these causes.

Jesus offered just such a testimony. Yet many people of his time questioned his credentials. He had to produce testimonies that accredited him: his works and miracles, John's identification of him as Saviour, the words of scripture that refer to him. He even embraced death to show how far he was willing to go for our sake. By his resurrection, the Father rendered the ultimate testimony.

How about us? How far are we willing to go to witness to our faith? How committed are we to take seriously the call of radical discipleship? We can begin by recognising those who offer a liberating message for us despite their physical imprisonment. Without risking our lives, we too can commit ourselves – in no matter how simple and quiet a way – to acts of mercy and compassion so that we can become messengers of God to others.

Thought for the day

"Our faith in the power of the cross and resurrection empowers us to live out the vision of God's new creation, where no one is subordinated or enslaved, but where free people take part in God's liberating project to build a true community and a new society." (The Ecumenical Association of Third World Theologians)

Prayer

Dear Lord, every day we hear of our brothers and sisters around the world who are suffering for their commitment to justice, peace and freedom. Trapped by a sense of helplessness, we may eventually become numb to these issues, worrying only about our own concerns. Revive us Lord; make our hearts burn within us so that we too can make a prophetic testimony.
Amen.

Fourth Friday of Lent

Where is he?

Ws 12:1, 12-22; Ps 33:16, 18, 19-21, 23; Jn 11:18-20

After his brothers had left for the festival, Jesus went up as well; however, he did not go openly, but secretly. The Jewish authorities were looking for him at the festival, "Where is he?" they asked.

(John 7:10)

Where is he? During Jesus' lifetime on earth, many people asked this question – the religious and military authorities, his friends and disciples, even his parents.

It is a question that still comes up on many occasions and in many places in our world today. In the context of contemporary social problems, for example, countless victims of oppression, racism, rejection and alienation are looking for Jesus, just as the Jewish slaves in Egypt searched for Yahweh in the pre-Exodus times. Modern-day disciples look for him as they struggle to interpret his call within the context of modern society.

The question is on the lips of victims of political repression; of journalists and human rights advocates who risk imprisonment; of prisoners of conscience whose lives are threatened; of trade union leaders whose rights are being violated. At moments of despair and helplessness they ask: where is he?

It is on the lips of overseas contract workers from the poor countries of Asia and Africa who work in the Middle East, Europe and the rich East and Southeast Asian countries; of all who suffer abuse at the hands of their employers.

In one recent case, however, no-one needed to ask "where is he?" – for it was clear that Jesus was present. In June 1996, 300 African refugees sought sanctuary in the church of St Bernard in Paris, helped by the parish priest, Henri Coinde. The French government declared them illegal immigrants and eventually ended the standoff by breaking into the church. Supporters outside the church resisted the police, shouting: "Solidarity with the *sans-papiers*! Liberty! Equality!"

Despite the eventual deportation of many of the Africans, the great support shown to them testified to the presence of Jesus. Wherever in the world people of different colours, class, sex, age or political orientations join hands to work for justice, peace and freedom – there, too, is Jesus Christ.

Thought for the day

"To love another person is to see the face of God." (From the musical *Les Miserables*)

Prayer

Lord, in our moments of despair, hopelessness, and alienation, we fail to discover your presence in us. After a while, we stop looking, and instead find other ways of coping with our anxieties. Lord, don't give up on us. Revive our faith in you. Shake us, disturb our apathy, and open our hearts to the people who have far better reasons than us to feel despair.

Amen.

Fourth Saturday of Lent

Power play

Jr 11:18-20; Ps 7:2-3, 9-12; Jn 7:40-52

Nicodemus – the same man who had come to Jesus earlier – said to them, "But surely the Law does not allow us to pass judgement on a man without giving him a hearing and discovering what he is about?" To this they answered, "Are you a Galilean too? Go into the matter, and see for yourself; prophets do not come out of Galilee."

(John 7:50-52)

To be a Church of the poor is the vision of many local Churches in the world today. This is especially true for dioceses in the developing countries of Latin America, Africa and Asia. It is also being echoed in dioceses of rich countries who find themselves with an increasing number of poor people in their midst.

The Church in the Philippines, for example, decided six years ago to embrace this vision. Church workers involved in building basic ecclesial communities in the countryside among landless peasants, plantation farm workers and fishing communities have had little difficulty in bringing local people to grips with this concept.

In fact, it was the poor themselves who helped to formulate what a Church of the poor is all about when some dioceses began to take the idea seriously during the Marcos dictatorship days. Sadly, this led to many Christian communities being threatened and harassed.

However, when church workers in urban parishes brought this concept to the attention of the richer sections of society they encountered resentment and a lack of understanding. This is not surprising, in light of the gap between the experiences of the rich and the poor. As in the time of Jesus, it seems that the rich and powerful often find it much harder to be open to the Gospel, very few being willing to embrace the consequences of its message.

This is why Nicodemus stands out as a very interesting character in the gospels. In today's text, we see him coming to Jesus' defence despite considerable risks. Why did this person, who belonged to a powerful group like the Pharisees, seek Jesus? What drew him to Jesus, what was it in Jesus' actions and words that touched him?

It is possible for us to follow Jesus and be part of the Church of the poor, whatever our social background. But first, like Nicodemus, we must find time to know Jesus and to understand the kingdom that he proclaims. We must also be willing not to rely on the luxuries that money and power bring to our lives and instead strive for a life lived in simplicity, humility, and service to others.

Thought for the day

"There is no conversion before God without a conversion before others, especially the poor. Conversion means sharing. A person who does not share is not within the justice of God." (Jose Ignacio Vigil)

Prayer

Lord, we want to understand what our role is in building the reign of God. We may wish we could meet you in person, like Nicodemus did; nevertheless, we remember that even amongst those who met you, many refused your call. Help us to transcend our comfortable lifestyles and become willing to take the risks involved in embracing the cross.

Amen.

Sheila Cassidy
Fifth week of Lent

Fifth Sunday of Lent

God's promises

Jr 31:31-34; Ps 50:3-4, 12-15; Heb 5:7-9; Jn 12:20-30

This is the covenant I will make with the House of Israel when those days arrive – it is the Lord who speaks. Deep within them I will plant my Law, writing it on their hearts. Then I will be their God and they shall be my people.

(Jeremiah 31:33-34)

Why is it, I wonder, that most people have such a jaundiced view of poor old Jeremiah? I love him because he is so very human, protesting weakly when God calls him to be a prophet that he is only a child, not really fitted to do the job.

What Jeremiah didn't know, however, was that God likes calling the unsuitable, he chooses the weak and makes them strong, makes the stutterer articulate precisely so that it can be seen that it is he (or she!), God, who is at work in that person.

In this passage, God, through Jeremiah, announces a new covenant with the House of Israel, a very different one from that which was ratified amid the pyrotechnics of Mount Sinai. At this point it is worth reading through the Sinai story again (Exodus:19) because it highlights the contrast between the old covenant and God's promise to Jeremiah.

At Sinai, God dictated the Ten Commandments to Moses, and Moses wrote them down upon tablets of stone. This was God's law, and, out of fear, the people of Israel promised to do as they were told.

I find it odd and rather sad that I, as a child in a convent school, was told all about the Ten Commandments but nothing about the later covenant given to Jeremiah. In this passage we again meet the God who loves his people so much that he decides to write his message in their hearts, to instil into all men and women that intuitive knowledge that we call conscience, that knowledge of what is right and wrong, that we must cleave to the truth and shelter the widow and the orphan.

Perhaps God realised that the engraving on the stone tablets would become indecipherable as the years passed, that they might be broken or lost, and so was determined to write his law where it would never be lost, so that we might be his people, and he, our God.

Thought for the day

God's law is written in my heart: to read it I must look deeply, listen intently, be still and know that God is God, that he made me and loves me just as I am.

Prayer

Lord of my heart,
teach me to be still,
to listen, to learn,
so I may speak in your name.

Fifth Monday of Lent

Harlots and hypocrites

Dn 13:1-9, 15-17, 19-30, 33-62; Ps 22; Jn 8:1-11

"And now have I to die, innocent as I am of everything their malice has invented against me?"

(Daniel 13:43)

He looked up and said, "Woman, where are they? Has no-one condemned you?" "No-one, sir," she replied. "Neither do I condemn you," said Jesus.

(John 8:10-11)

What lesson does the Church want us to draw from the stories in today's readings, I wonder? My guess is that the moral that I will draw is a very different one from that which my Victorian ancestors would have chosen.

Here we have two women, one a virtuous wife, one an adultress, both accused of having sex outside of marriage. Susannah, mercifully, was cleared by Daniel's shrewd advocacy, but the woman caught committing adultery would have died if Jesus had not intervened. It's all rather hard to believe, isn't it, when in our own day there is talk of legalising brothels and bored married couples have "key parties" in which home keys are muddled up and partners are swapped for the night. At the same time, there are still places in the world where adultery is a crime which is punishable by death.

These stories, I think, are not so much a plea for purity and sexual forbearance as a protest against hypocrisy amongst these accusers who are all, after all, church-going people. Jesus managed to get rid of the scribes and the Pharisees who were ready to condemn the adultress, by writing in the dust. So what did he write? Legend has it that he wrote the hidden sexual sins of the Pharisees, reminding them that they were no better than the woman they were accusing and shaming them into silence.

My guess is that God dislikes hypocrites a great deal more than he does harlots. In the gospels, the harlot is forgiven but the hypocrite is not.

Sexual impropriety has been with us since time began and will surely be with us until the last lovers kiss. Whilst this is something for which each person must eventually stand accountable before God, how much better it would be if our newspapers focused less on the activities of consenting adults and more on issues of hunger, injustice and violence.

Thought for the day

Could we throw the first stone?

Prayer

Lord, we are a sinful lot, every man and woman of us. Give us the strength to be humble, to repent, and to work for justice, healing and love.

Fifth Tuesday of Lent

Nourished by prayer

Nb 21:4-9; Ps 101:2-3, 16-21; Jn 8:21-30

On the way the people lost patience. They spoke against God and against Moses. "Why did you bring us out of Egypt to die in this wilderness? For there is neither bread nor water here; we are sick of this unsatisfying food."

Why, I wonder, do the more ambitious of us desire to be leaders: head girl, member of parliament, chief executive. Is it because we lust for power, or for extra money, or are we just born with this curious drive to compete?

If we do achieve a position of leadership, however, we soon learn that it is pretty lonely. Moses learnt this early on, for the Israelites were always complaining, always asking for more than God had given them. No sooner were they safely through the Red Sea, than they started murmuring against God, saying to Moses:

"Why did we not die at Yahweh's hand in the land of Egypt? Then we were able to sit down to pans of meat and could eat bread to our hearts content? As it is, you have brought us into this wilderness to starve this whole company to death."

God, however, had no intention of starving his chosen people to death so he sent them special iron rations in the form of manna, a curious powdery substance that coated the ground after the morning dew lifted.

A Jesuit friend of mine likens our experience of prayer to the Jews' experience of manna. It is strange stuff, prayer, not really the sort of thing you'd expect to sustain you on a journey, and yet it does. Like the Israelites, we must gather our "manna" each morning; it can't be stored, but must be collected fresh every day. It's unlike anything else, but if we take it in faith, we will have strength to finish our trek through the wilderness.

The problem with prayer is the same as the problem with manna: it can be pretty tasteless and we get bored with it. In today's reading, the Israelites complain of the "unsatisfactory food", just as we might mutter "I can't be bothered to pray today, I don't seem to get anything out of it."

We long for prayer to be sweet and comforting, as the Israelites longed for the roast lamb and the pomegranates of Egypt. Prayer can seem dry and boring, but if we persist, it will keep us going until we reach the next oasis and rejoice again in God's more palpable gifts.

Thought for the day

Without the manna of prayer we will indeed die in the wilderness.

Prayer

Lord our God, give us the courage and discipline to walk the dark ways of faith so that we may see your face.

Going through the mangle

Dn 3:14-20, 24, 25, 28; Dn 3:52-56; Jn 8:31-42

"If you make my work your home
you will indeed be my disciples,
you will learn the truth
and the truth will make you free."

(John 8:31-32)

When I was around forty, I entered a monastic convent in search of a way of life which would lead to union with God. I thought I knew all about monastic life, but I was quite unprepared for the reality of being a middle-aged novice.

Sometimes I think the only thing that kept me sane was a poster showing an extremely unhappy rag doll being put through a mangle, with the caption: "The Truth will set you free, but first it will make you miserable." Looking at this poster I would grit my teeth and mutter: "*nil carborundum illegitimi*": don't let the rascals grind you down. Alas, the harder I tried the worse things became, and eventually I was asked to leave because I was so unhappy.

Not a little put out, and determined to show them, I decided to be a hermit. For the first couple of weeks I found the life very satisfactory. I rose early, said my prayers, and drove off to Mass. After Mass I would have a coffee, then go shopping, and then buy fish and chips and eat them meditatively on the riverbank. After six weeks however, I ran out of money and was forced to seek work as a doctor (medicine being my only marketable skill).

To my great surprise, and with much inner laughter, I discovered what I had forgotten: that I have a very powerful call to medicine and that I am quite good at it. As I walked down the hospital corridor humming a little song, I realised the true meaning of my mangle poster. The convent was my mangle: it nearly squeezed the life out of me but it taught me a very important fact: that I was profoundly unsuited to the religious life.

After twenty years imagining myself pursued by the Hound of Heaven, this truth was immensely freeing, for I realised that God wanted me to be myself and not try to fit myself into another woman's corset.

Although this is my story, it illustrates an important general truth: that we do not have to travel to the ends of the earth to find God, because wherever we happen to be – in the kitchen, in the office – he has already found us.

Thought for the day

If the Son makes you free, you will be free indeed.

Prayer

Lord, I want to be
Joan of Arc
Mother Teresa
Ignatius of Loyola ...
but it seems I can only
be me.
Will that do?

Fifth Thursday of Lent

Locking God up

Gn 17:3-9; Ps 104:4-9; Jn 8:51-59

"I will establish my Covenant between myself and you, and your descendants after you, a Covenant in perpetuity, to be your God and the God of your descendants after you."

(Genesis 17:8)

Abram, the faithful man sent out into the wilderness, is an iconic figure for us all. Like us, Abram – now named Abraham by God – walked trembling into the unknown, with nothing but God's covenant to keep him warm. But Abraham was to learn, as we must, that God's promise to be with us is better than cloak or compass. God's word is his bond: if we keep his law, he will walk with us.

God doesn't promise us that the sun will always shine or that he will not take away his gifts: he threatened to take away Abraham's beloved son Isaac. The notion that we can get on God's "good" side and escape harm is extremely naive: as the great Rhineland mystic Meister Eckhart said, "God often lets his friends fall sick" – he pulls the mat from under their feet, to emphasise their dependence on him.

My own experience of God's covenant presence is that I am usually aware of it in retrospect rather than at the time. It is the nature of suffering that we feel desolate and abandoned: if we were aware of God with us, then we would not really be suffering. Like Jacob, we wrestle all night with a stranger: with pain, temptation, anger, and then when the sun rises we say in surprise: "Hey! The Lord was here and I never realised it."

The Benedictine monk Cyprian Smith has written of the *Way of Paradox*, and the Jesuit Gerard W. Hughes of the *God of Surprises*. It is good to reflect upon these titles and realise that our God is neither tame or predictable. We can rely upon God but we cannot forecast what he will do. The Indian Jesuit writer and preacher Antony de Mello once said "Empty out your tea-cup God!" If your idea of God is too small, then get rid of it!

That, I believe, is one of the great secrets of the spiritual life. Once we stop shutting God in the tabernacle and allow him inside us, then we will glimpse him more often. No wonder Jesus drove the Pharisees mad: they kept God safely locked away in the temple and couldn't bear the idea of him being present in an itinerant preacher. Poor Pharisees: they thought they'd got rid of him when they saw him die on the cross; they didn't know that you can't kill God.

Thought for the day

"Empty out your tea-cup God."

Prayer

Holy God
holy and strong
holy and deathless
have mercy on us.

Fifth Friday of Lent

God made me this way

Jer 20:10-13; Ps 17:2-7; Jn 10:31-32

All those who used to be my friends
watched for my downfall.

(Jeremiah 20:10)

In today's readings we see the familiar pattern of the persecution of the prophet. Why do prophets always upset people?

The American writer Fredrick Bueckner says: "No-one ever invited a prophet home to dinner more then once." Prophets make us uncomfortable because they get under our defences: they see through our smart clothes to our grubby underwear, reveal that our pious hypocrisy covers a man or woman who is as weak and greedy as anyone else.

I think this is an important point: Jesus didn't make fun of sinners, only of pompous hypocrites who thought they were better than anyone else. How we religious people long to be holier than everyone else! Holier than the atheists, the Buddhists, the Hindus, the Taoists and all the rest. Why?

Perhaps the problem is that we think God only likes holy people. We forget Jesus's repeated message that his mission was to the lost sheep, the poor confused sinners, not to the spiritually wealthy and self-righteous. We should be happy that we are sinners, that we are weak and lost, because we will ride on the shepherd's shoulders, while the holy people walk!

It has taken me years to realise God loves me as I am. All the years that I was aspiring to be Joan of Arc, Teresa of Avila and John of the Cross rolled into one, I thought that if only I could be pure and holy and ascetic, I would be OK in God's eyes. But slowly, over many years of psychotherapy and spiritual guidance, I have come to realise that I am the way that I am because God made me that way.

Like everyone else, I am a product of my genes and my childhood upbringing, of my fate and my fortune. The passionate lust for beautiful possessions which makes me fill my home with things I do not need is part of me. I long to travel light, to have just a few possessions, but instead I have a hundred teddy bears and countless sweaters. But I also do many things which I know are of God, so I do what I can, and wait for the wheat and tares to be separated at harvest time.

Thought for the day

Be patient with yourself and know that the Lord of the Harvest loves you as you are.

Prayer

Lord of the Harvest,
sow me as seed
to make food for your people.

Fifth Saturday of Lent

Love is stronger than fear

Ezk 37:21-28; Jer 31:10-13; Jn 11:45-57

Then the chief priests and Pharisees called a meeting. "Here is this man working all these signs," they said, "and what action are we taking? If we let him go on in this way everybody will believe in him and the Romans will come and destroy the Holy Place and our nation."

(John 11:47-8)

Today's reading from St John's gospel follows on from the story of when Jesus raised Lazarus from the dead. No wonder the religious people of the day were scared of him: he challenged everything they held sacred. They believed that the God of their fathers was safely contained in the temple, and here was this man claiming to be God's son. Worse than that, he was working miracles, amazing cures, and now he had even raised a man from the dead.

Faced by such wonders, who would believe them any more, and if they lost control over the people, the Romans would surely make them suffer.

The elders were in agreement: something must be done. Then Caiaphas, the high priest of the year, spoke up: "You don't seem to have grasped the situation at all," he said. His real message was this: can't you see that the only solution is to kill this man? Being a high priest, he phrased it more subtly: "You fail to see that it is better for one man to die for the people than for the whole nation to be destroyed."

"There is nothing new under the sun", said Ecclesiastes cynically, and we cannot but agree. Two thousand years later, the high priests and elders of our own day – the politicians and chief executives – still plot together to remove a particular man or woman who presents a threat to the security of the state. Why else did Archbishop Romero die, or Martin Luther King, or Steve Biko?

Perhaps it's easier to enter the mind of Jesus if we think about more recent martyrs. Although Oscar Romero took precautions, he knew that if the authorities wanted to kill him, they would. He must surely have been frightened, but his love of his people and a holy anger against oppression urged him on.

It was the same for Jesus. He knew they were out to get him, so he kept out of their way. But he knew too, that he had a mission to accomplish, so love overrode prudence and he went up to Jerusalem. Next week we hear that story again, lest we forget that God's son lived among us, that he ate and drank and laughed with us, and that he laid down his life because he loved us.

Thought for the day

Remember that Jesus was scared too.

Prayer

Lord, I'm scared of death, of pain, of humiliation: give me the strength I need to do your will.

Jim O'Keefe
Holy week

Passion / Palm Sunday

The real crucifix

Mk 11:1-10; Is 50:4-7; Ph 2:6-11; Mk 14:1-15:47

His state was divine,
yet Christ Jesus did not cling
to his equality with God
but emptied himself
to assume the condition of a slave,
and became as men are;
and being as all men are,
he was humbler yet,
even to accepting death,
death on a cross.

(Philippians 2:6-8)

They say that a young woman went into a jeweller's shop to buy a cross and chain for her fiancé. She was told that if she wanted a cross "with the little man on it" the cost would be £15, but if she wanted one "without the little man on it" the cost would only be £12.

There is a real danger that the cross has been domesticated. There is no such thing as a "nice crucifix". The cross is a symbol of torture and death and so it is no wonder that our Christian sisters and brothers who lived in the first two centuries did not use the cross as a symbol. For them the cross stood for the shameful means whereby slaves were put to death. There are no drawings or carvings of the cross on the walls of the catacombs in Rome. Today, although we use it as a symbol, we are more likely to ignore its true meaning.

Jesus always addressed the reality facing him. He did not climb the hill opposite the city of Jerusalem and run away into the desert after the Last Supper. He discouraged his disciples from fighting on his behalf in the Garden. He did not ask for mercy during his trial. He put himself in the hands of his Father and never took advantage of his "divinity".

The cross symbolises the risk Jesus took, his commitment to and love of the Father. He lived through that experience of Golgotha as someone who was powerless, voiceless, marginalised, stigmatised and alienated. He did not "cling to his equality with God" – he reinforced his identity with deeply flawed human beings.

Holy Week can be a time for us to ponder our own power, what it is we cling to, where we keep our treasure buried. It can be a time to wonder about our obsession with status, possessions, privacy and being in control; but it can also be a time to allow the Spirit of the Suffering Servant to take over more of our decisions and plans.

Thought for the day

Why not spend five minutes each day gazing at the crucifix, letting the Lord speak to you about the risk he took in not clinging to his equality with God.

Prayer

Lord Jesus, open our eyes that we may see our own yearning for safety and security. Help us to take the risk of getting closer to those on the margins in our world so that we can be filled with your Spirit.

Amen.

Monday of Holy Week

Reckless behaviour

Is 42:1-7; Ps 26:1-3, 13-14; Jn 12:1-11

Mary brought in a pound of very costly ointment, pure nard, and with it anointed the feet of Jesus, wiping them with her hair.

(John 12:3)

Mary Magdalene is one of the many provocative women in the gospels. These women provoke Jesus into saying or doing things which reveal more of his true self. Mary comes into the gathering and anoints the feet of Jesus with costly scented ointment which comes from the mountains in northern India. She wipes his feet with her hair. What a dramatic story!

Perhaps Jesus was so touched by this reckless and generous gesture that he was influenced by it when he washed the feet of his own disciples during the Last Supper. The washing of his disciples' feet became the symbol of ultimate service for others. In John's gospel this gesture takes the place of the breaking of bread and the sharing of the one cup. Mary may have taught Jesus something profound, and he was humble enough to learn.

Mary was poor. Not in the sense that she had no money – she had, she had bought very expensive ointment – but she was truly poor. She was a true disciple of Jesus, focusing entirely on his needs and the inevitability of his death and what that death would mean. She was not distracted by public opinion nor by the apparently politically correct mutterings of the false disciple Judas Iscariot. For Mary there was only one thing that mattered – showing her love for the one person in her life who accepted her totally and without question.

Her response was indeed generous and reckless, rather like the love God has for each of us. On this occasion she acted like one of the children so beloved by Jesus. She allowed herself to be influenced by matters of the heart and not just of the head. Jesus may well have uttered a silent prayer of thanks that his Father had once again revealed the important thing to the childlike person, rather than the correct person. The false disciple provoked the comment: "You have the poor with you always", probably because Jesus knew that there would always be people who would strive to be rich.

Thought for the day

In the decisions I make today, will I be more of a childlike, true disciple, influenced by matters of the heart, or a correct, false disciple, looking out for my own status and security?

Prayer

Lord Jesus, friend of the poor, help me to become more open to the presence of your Spirit in children and those without power. May your spirit of generosity lead me to become a true disciple.

Amen.

Tuesday of Holy Week

Betrayal

Is 49:1-6; Ps 70:1-6, 15, 17; Jn 13:21-33, 36-38

"I tell you most solemnly, one of you will betray me."
The disciples looked at one another, wondering which
he meant.

(John 13:2-3)

The Last Supper must have been a gathering of very tense people. Jesus was aware that the authorities were after him. He had said and done enough to provoke them into violent action. The meal had been arranged in secret. He may well have realised that this was the last time he would share a meal with his close friends and followers on earth. Jesus would need this closeness and companionship to give him the strength to face the future. He probably also realised that with his capture, his followers would quickly disperse. There would have been a sense of urgency in the air.

In the middle of it all he declared that one of the group would betray him. This must have sent shock waves through those who heard the comment. They had done so much together, travelled so far and witnessed great events together. Yet one would betray him.

The betrayer triggered off a train of events which led to the death of Jesus. The betrayer colluded with those who wanted to destroy Jesus, those who could not tolerate his witness to forgiveness, inclusiveness and the call to bring the fullness of life to all women and men in the world.

Most of us could not imagine ourselves betraying anyone, but we need to be careful. How easy it is to live in the rich

North and collude with companies that do not respect their workers in developing countries. How easy it is to become immune to the fact that one child in three born in the United Kingdom is born into poverty, or that eighteen million people in our world will die of hunger this year. How easy it is to betray our brothers and sisters through silent and uncritical collusion.

No wonder Pope John Paul II insists in his letter *Sollicitudo Rei Socialis* that the structures of sin in our society are the result of our "laziness, fear or conspiracy of silence". In other words, we betray those in our world who are weak and fragile when we live untouched by their suffering. We need not look around to see who is doing the betraying, we need only look in the mirror.

Thought for the day

We may not be traitors, but we can betray one another through our silence and lack of concern.

Prayer

Loving Lord, give us the eyes to see the needs of others, ears to hear their voice calling out, and give us the courage to change.

Amen.

Wednesday of Holy Week

Handing over

Is 50:4-9; Ps 68:8-10, 21-22, 31, 33-34; Mt 26:14-25

Then one of the Twelve, the man called Judas Iscariot, went to the chief priests and said, "What are you prepared to give me if I hand him over to you?" They paid him thirty silver pieces, and from that moment he looked for an opportunity to betray him.

(Matthew 26:14-16)

We all like to imagine ourselves as compassionate people, feeling concern for the plight of our sisters and brothers here and throughout the world. We cannot imagine ourselves not being touched by the circumstances in which they live. We feel shocked and horrified when children are killed by others their own age, when women are violently attacked in their own homes, when people suffer from terrorist attacks, famine or war.

But the word compassion implies more than feeling deeply concerned about something, it demands that we stand alongside the sufferer and be physically affected by their plight. Some people say that the Greek word for compassion captures the physical, visceral experience of a woman giving birth to a child. This is the extent of compassion, it implies a driving urge to be near and be of service.

To hand someone over for money is the exact opposite of compassion. This is a total refusal to stand alongside or to suffer with another. To hand someone over in this way is a denial of common humanity. This is not, however, the same as sharing the care of a child or a relation with special needs with people who are gifted and specially trained to care. This is not a "handing over" in the sense of a betrayal, but is the wise acknowledgement that we are limited and need help to cope with a parent living with Alzheimers disease or a friend living with AIDS. This is about harnessing the skills and gifts in the community for the benefit of someone who is in real need.

Prayer is the essence of compassion. When we pray for the child in need, the friend with mental health problems, the parent with dementia or the friend with AIDS, we are actually asking God to help us appreciate the world from their perspective.

Our prayer will help us feel something of the isolation, fear, anxiety or helplessness of the person in need. We are not "handing them over for money" – we are handing them to the Lord and asking the Lord to help us share their perspective. If we feel differently, then we may learn to act differently – compassionately.

Thought for the day

When we pray for other people, we are inviting God to help us change, to see things in a very different way from now on. Once we choose to help the person in need, we cannot really avoid being changed ourselves.

Prayer

Loving God, give us the imagination and energy we need to work for the things we pray for.

Amen.

Maundy Thursday

Broken people

Ex 12:1-8, 11-14; Ps 115:12-13, 15-18; 1 Co 11:23-26; Jn 13:1-15

On the same night that he was betrayed, the Lord Jesus took some bread, and thanked God for it and broke it, and he said, "This is my body, which is for you; do this as a memorial of me."

(1 Corinthians 11:23-24)

St John tells us that the Last Supper was a celebration of the Passover – the memorial of the escape of the Hebrews from slavery in Egypt. The liberating event we call the Exodus took place in a context of slavery, oppression and violence. The Last Supper of Jesus was the last event in his life before he went on to suffer betrayal, personal anguish, arrest, isolation, torture and death.

Have we not domesticated our liturgy in such a way that we have lost the urgency and raw human experience in the lives of our sisters and brothers? Both the Exodus and the Last Supper are events surrounded by deeply human emotions and decisions.

Some people in the Third World have said that we in the rich North have forfeited the right to celebrate the Eucharist because we refuse to be moved by the brokenness in the lives of others. This is a shocking statement, but it can make us think.

Jesus gave his very self in the Eucharist. He gave us himself as one who insisted on including the outcast. He did not just heal the woman with the haemorrhage, he freed her from permanent impurity and enabled her to play her full part in the community. The same is true with lepers, those who were possessed, the physically ill and public sinners. Jesus was committed to inclusiveness.

As we assemble for the Mass of the Lord's Supper we are committing ourselves to perpetuate this memorial. The broken body of the Lord is present in the brokenness of every one of us. By receiving the broken body of the Lord we are pledging ourselves to stand alongside the brokenness of others – and to allow them to stand by our brokenness also. As we receive from the one cup, we pledge ourselves to work for justice, for unity and reconciliation.

It is no wonder that Pope John Paul II asks in his apostolic letter *Tertio Millennio Adveniente*, "how can we fail to lay greater emphasis on the Church's preferential option for the poor and the outcast?"

Our commitment to this "preferential option" is central to the memorial we celebrate tonight.

Thought for the day

We live in a broken world; our sharing in the Eucharist shows our commitment to help bring about the Kingdom of the Lord.

Prayer

Loving God, your son Jesus gives himself to us in the Eucharist. Help us to become less afraid of the brokenness in ourselves and others, and more willing to work for the unity and peace he called for.

Amen.

Good Friday

How close?

Is 52:13-53:12; Ps 30:2, 6, 12-13, 15-17, 25; Heb 4:14-16; 5:7-9; Jn 18:1-19:42

Near the cross of Jesus stood his mother and his mother's sister, Mary the wife of Clopas, and Mary of Magdala.

(John 19:25)

The gospel writers place Mary of Magdala as the most consistent presence at the foot of the cross. The public sinner whose life was transformed through her relationship with Jesus, the woman who later became the first witness of the Resurrection, stood as near as anyone to the foot of the cross.

How close would we stand to the cross? What drew Mary of Magdala to take the risk to stay so close to the execution of Jesus? Will the same risky love urge us to be profoundly moved or seriously influenced by the plight of other people?

As Mary looked up into the eyes of her Saviour, she would see the plight of the useless, the suspect, the abused, the powerless, the oppressed, the despised – and she still stayed there. She stayed close to the man who was dying because he was incapable of excluding anyone from his influence and his imagination. For us, this much goodness is too threatening, we cannot stand too close to it.

Most of Jesus' other friends have been distancing themselves from him since his arrest in the garden. In Mark's gospel we have the simple story of the disciple who left his cloak in the garden as he ran away naked. He gave up everything he had to follow Jesus and then gave up everything he had to get away from him. That wonderful man Peter denied Jesus three times – but at least he was near enough to hear the cock crow and humble enough to weep copiously because of his weakness.

But Mary stayed close, and leaves each of us with the question: how close would we have stood? The work of art in St Peter's in Rome that we call the Pietà illustrates the helplessness of Mary the mother of Jesus as she held his body in death. She is as distraught as any mother would be holding her dead child. But she was there.

How close will we allow ourselves to get to the desolation of others? Can we stand close to others in a gentle, humble way, even keeping to the shadows so that we are not intrusive? Can we act decisively to come close to the person of the crucified Lord in those around us who suffer? Can we take Mary of Magdala as our model and not be afraid of our own weakness?

Thought for the day

Try and keep in touch with your own internal responses and reactions to the news about the struggles taking place in other people's lives.

Prayer

Loving God, it can be very difficult to stay close, not to run away from the things we find hard. Help us to embrace our own weaknesses and thereby become less afraid of the weaknesses of others. We ask this through Christ our Lord. Amen.

Easter Sunday

Celebrate!

Ac 10:34, 37-43; Ps 117:1-2, 16-17, 22-23; Col 3:1-4; Jn 20:1-9

"He has risen, he is not here ... " And the women came out and ran away from the tomb because they were frightened out of their wits; and they said nothing to a soul, for they were afraid.

(Mark 16:6-8)

The reality of the resurrection emerges out of the deeply-felt emotions of the previous few days. The women are "frightened out of their wits," they run away and say nothing because they are afraid. Who can blame them? It is only when the risen Lord begins to move back into their lives that they allow themselves the joy and hope that Jesus still lives among them.

The dawn is gradual. There is the tiniest spot of light emerging from the slight yellow-grey line on the horizon. Once the spot of light is clear, it quickly enlarges to throw huge swathes of bright light across the sky. The sun emerges to warm and cajole, to encourage new life and growth.

The realisation of the resurrection of Jesus dawned slowly. Those who witnessed and heard were not sure; there was testing-out and denial. Gradually the truth gains a strong foothold. The Lord meets his friends and gives them yet another chance to follow him. Yet they are still frightened and it takes the explosive power of Pentecost for their fears to be driven away and their full freedom in the Lord to come to fruition.

We certainly are the Easter People, and alleluia is indeed our song. But it is a slow process and we all move at different rates. We must celebrate glimpses of the light with music and colour and movement and great joy. We must celebrate the presence of the risen Lord in our friendships, the commitments we see around us, the freedom which is being won for at least some people in the world.

Any act which breaks through prejudice and fear, any new bond of friendship across cultural divides or ghetto traditions, any project which helps to bring the fullness of life to anyone, is a glimpse of the dawn of the resurrection. These things must be enjoyed and seen as candles or even beacons lighting up the Way.

The celebration of Easter roots us in the idealism of the Jubilee. We have to learn to read the good signs around us as instances of Jubilee. Perhaps we should spend any Easter holidays we have "spotting the Jubilee", and once we have spotted it, celebrate it with immense joy and thanksgiving.

Thought for the day

Enjoy it! Get into the habit of seeing the good things around us as instances of the risen Lord showing us what the Jubilee is about.

Prayer

This is what we are about.
We plant the seeds that one day will grow,
We water seeds already planted,
Knowing that they hold future promise.
We lay foundations that will need further development.
We provide yeast that produces effects
Far beyond our capabilities.

We may never see the end results,
But that is the difference
Between the master builder and the worker.
We are workers not master builders,
Ministers not messiahs.
We are prophets of a future not our own.
(Oscar Romero)